SEX & LOVE

WHEN YOU'RE

SINGLE
AGAIN

SEX & LOVE
WHEN YOU'RE
SINGLE
AGAIN

THOMAS F. JONES

A Division of Thomas Nelson Publishers
Nashville

Published in Nashville, Tennessee, by Oliver-Nelson Books, a division of Thomas Nelson, Inc., Publishers, and distributed in Canada by Lawson Falle, Ltd., Cambridge, Ontario.

Unless otherwise noted, the Bible version used in this publication is THE NEW KING JAMES VERSION. Copyright © 1979, 1980, 1982, Thomas Nelson, Inc., Publishers.

Scripture quotations marked NIV are taken from the HOLY BIBLE: NEW INTERNATIONAL VERSION. Copyright © 1973, 1978, 1984 by the International Bible Society. Used by permission of Zondervan Bible Publishers.

Names and events have been fictionalized to protect privacy.

Printed in the United States of America.

Library of Congress Cataloging-in-Publication Data

Jones, Thomas F., 1936–
    Sex and love when you're single again / Thomas F. Jones.
      p.   cm.
    ISBN 0-8407-9571-8
    1. Divorced people—United States—Sexual behavior. 2. Sexual
ethics—United States. I. Title.
HQ18.U5J66   1990
306.7'08'653—dc20
                                                90–34134
                                                  CIP

1 2 3 4 5 6 — 95 94 93 92 91 90

I would like to dedicate this book to the dearest friend
I have ever known, my wife, Reidun.

During the ten years of our relationship prior to our marriage in
1985, she demonstrated to me by the life she lived all of the
principles of love, friendship, and sexual balance of which I have
written. I am indebted to her for so much of what I have learned.
I honor her above all women, and I am forever grateful to God
for giving me such an undeserved gift.

Ten years ago, I wrote the following song for her. What I sought
to express to her then is truer today than when I wrote it.

Reidun, thank you. You make my heart sing!

You, my lovely sister,
You, my dearest friend,
God has given you to me
In the wisdom of His plan.
I am growing once again.

I can see the sun is shining
I can feel the warm rain on my skin
I can tell my heart is moving
I am growing once again.

I was empty, you filled my heart with love
I was lonely, you were my friend,
I was dying, you brought new life to me,
I am growing once again.

In the counsel of the Lord,
By the leading of His hand
God has given you to me
I am growing once again
I am growing once again.

Contents

Acknowledgments

There are countless others who have contributed to the writing of this book. My understanding of the journey of the person who is single again is so much deeper and broader than what I personally have experienced because I have known so many others who have been willing to share their stories with me. I want to thank them for their trust and their teaching.

Others have helped me more specifically. I greatly appreciate the encouragement which I have received from Bob Burns since he first invited me to participate in ministry to the divorced. He has often pointed me in directions of greater service and usefulness. He also read the manuscript and made many helpful suggestions.

I also want to thank Tom Whiteman, Sandy Harding, Marilyn Theys, and my wife, Reidun, who also took the time to read the manuscript and offer their constructive help.

Paul Malone deserves much thanks for his help in properly preparing the floppy disks and hard copies of the manuscript for the editors. I would have been in a lot of trouble without him.

And I very much appreciate the direction and assistance given to me by Victor Oliver and Lila Empson of Oliver-Nelson. Their expertise and personal guidance were always of great help. They were also remarkably patient and kind to a first-time author.

I give thanks to God for you all.

Introduction

I can still remember my first truly sexual experience. Her name was Linda, and we were fourth-grade classmates. I had known her for several years and had never once had a sexual thought about her. In fact, I don't think I had ever had a sexual thought. But when I was ten, something new and marvelous happened to me.

There had been a heavy snow, and all the neighborhood kids were sledding on our favorite hill. Linda had a brand-new sled and was showing it off. Then came the moment when she asked me if I would like to ride down the hill on her sled. I said that I would, and she flopped on the sled face down and said, "Hop on!"

I thought nothing of it at all, and so I hopped right on top of her. Off we went, bump, bump, bumpity, bump down that hill with me lying on Linda's back. Right then and there I discovered a whole new meaning and purpose for the universe.

Perhaps that sounds a bit overstated, but there is absolutely no question that a mysterious and wonderful new flame awakened in me, a flame that has never gone out or even dimmed. I have called that fateful sled ride a sexual experience, and that it was. Not that I experienced anything like a mature sexual feeling. I possessed no real sexual information (in that era ten-year-old boys were still innocent), and I was not physically stimulated (at least, not genitally). But something truly sexual occurred on that brand-new sled.

It was as if great wide doors had opened up in my mind and heart revealing broad vistas of new meaning for the terms *boy* and *girl*. For the first time ever I knew that there was a powerful and beautiful something alive inside me that could find its full explanation and solution only in nearness to a woman. I was a male, I needed a female, and that seemed like the most marvelous thing I had ever learned.

Many things have happened to me in the forty-odd years since Linda and I took that amazing sled ride in the snow. First of all I survived the traumatic fantasies of adolescence (most of which hung around much longer than adolescence). After that I got married and lived "happily ever after" for eleven years (during which time I would have considered myself to be sexually well informed and fulfilled [at least I had mastered the basics—three children were born]). But then my wife and I were divorced, and for the next fourteen years I walked alone. Now I am married again and feeling that I have graduated from the toughest school one could possibly attend—the School of Secondary Sexual Education.

That fourteen-year journey of being single again has been my greatest motivation to write this book. During that time, I learned new things about myself that I doubt I could have learned any other way. I learned that there were many ways in which I did not understand my sexual nature. I learned that I, who considered myself to be a strong, committed Christian man (and properly so, I think), was not fully in control of my sexual nature and, further, was fully capable of compromising my highest principles. I learned that the lessons of sexuality are not learned once and for all (like the multiplication tables) and then stored away in capsule form for future uses; rather, they are lessons that must be applied in new ways as life changes.

Sexuality took on new meanings for me as I struggled with my single state, meanings I would never have conceived of when I was single before. There was so much new thinking I was going to have to do, so much I would have to learn and relearn. I learned much during those years, but the most significant lesson was that God's grace is a wonderfully gentle and effective teacher. By that good grace of God I learned how to grow in sexual matters.

Beyond all those lessons, I learned that I was not alone. Many others in our society are struggling with the single-again experience precisely in the area of their sexuality. Many of them, like myself, are Christian (or, at least, people of generally high moral standards) and want sincerely to conduct themselves in responsible ways. Still, they are sexual beings, and their sexuality calls to them in ways that must have answers.

Biblically sound answers are not all that easy to find, however. If the church speaks to the issue of single sexuality at all, it usually speaks to adolescents. But the sexual struggles of persons who are single again are widely different from the struggles of young persons who have never married.

This book, then, is primarily for you who have been my fellow strugglers on the single-again road. I am writing out of deep compassion, for I know your struggles. I understand the emptiness and the loneliness that have been your constant companions. I understand the pain of not being touched anymore (often by your very best friends). I understand the guilt (whether real or imaginary) of normal sexual desire. I understand you because I have walked where you now walk. For what it may be worth, I care, and I offer you what I have learned.

May the same gracious God who has been so faithful and strong for me be your comfort and strength as well.

1

Do You Understand Sexuality?

I t has been forty-three years now since that remarkable sled ride with Linda. I am a grown man, considered to be mature, and the general presumption seems to be that people my age know all about sex and sexuality. I think this presumption is false. Even though we live in an age thought to be awakened and free in regard to sexuality, I continually discover that I am not alone in feeling my education in sexual matters has been incomplete and often downright incorrect.

It is certainly true that the kids of my generation were exposed to much more sexual information and openness than our parents had been. But we still grew up in sexual ignorance. Nobody really talked to us about sexuality. Oh, sure, there was a sprinkling of "sex talk" in many conversations, but such talk never became serious. No one ever sat down with us and explained anything sexual in a responsible and meaningful way.

Generally speaking, our parents did not talk to us about sexuality. I do not mean to put them down. Our parents were children of their own generation with their own struggles and hang-ups. Most of our parents did not believe it was proper to talk to children about such topics. The only thing that I can remember my father saying to me of an explicit sexual nature was a warning about the possible dangers of intimacy with a girlfriend (I was twenty-one years old at the time!).

The schools also failed us, except for offering a required health course. The book for the course included a chapter on the reproductive system, which contained very useful information. We learned the facts about the sexual anatomy and the reproductive cycle and even a few practical things about venereal disease and contraception. Those things were helpful, but I appreciated most of all having an adult stand there in front of us all and admit that he knew about sex! Up until then I wasn't really sure adults knew about it. It just felt so good to have a teacher come right out and use the terms of sexuality in an open way and treat us as if those were matters we needed to know about. But as important as that one chapter in health class was, it certainly wasn't enough.

It wasn't enough because there is far more to sexuality than the physical mechanics. In school they talked only about the biology of sex. They had nothing to say about the meaning of sex, the morality of sex, or the various roles that sex may have in a person's development. School taught us, by omission, that the only facts about sexuality were physical facts. But you had the deep and certain feeling that there were other facts you should know. If others knew those other facts, however, they weren't talking.

I don't suppose that I have to tell you how much the church had to say on the topic of sexuality. The leaders said nothing at all. To be sure, there was a general sense that the violation of the Seventh Commandment was looked upon with great disfavor. You got the idea in church that sexuality was capable of producing a great amount of evil and suffering, and woe be unto the youngster who dared think about it very much. In fact, you easily felt that if you did think about it much (as I certainly did), there was probably something evil about you. You certainly did not get positive instruction about the basic goodness of sexuality as part of God's holy and perfect creation. You were not taught to affirm the spiritual value of your sexuality. And you were not given any practical help with all of the Gordian knots that a normal teenager was seeking to untie. On those points the church was silent (at least in our hearing).

I have always looked back on my early years and considered it remarkable that the first adult voice I heard speaking positively about sexuality was that of Hugh Hefner. Not my parents, not my school, and not the church, but Hugh Hefner, the publisher of *Playboy*. What a commentary on that age! I was fourteen years old when Hefner began to publish his magazine. Boy, did he get my attention! Not merely because of the pictures. He was talking to us. Hefner began by asking the questions that we were all asking. What about the meaning of sexuality? What about morality? How do you establish moral standards for sexuality? And how do you answer the complex questions sexuality poses? We looked at the pictures, for sure, but we also read the "Playboy Philosophy" and wondered why no one else was speaking openly on the urgent subject.

Deep inside I think that all of us boys really wondered whether we were getting a fair shake from Hefner (I wonder what the girls were thinking). Certainly his questions had some authenticity. But the general moral tone of our homes and our perception of the church's sexual message as negative were too strong for most of us to simply accept Hefner without caution.

Then there were the real girls we knew. Real girls were so different from the pinups in the magazines. The pinups just stood there without their clothes and smiled at you. Real girls kept their clothes on and didn't always smile (at least, not at me). Real girls could talk, too, and they never talked about sex (at least, not with me).

When we started dating, sex was the last thing we ever talked about. It was on our minds. (I assume it was on the girl's mind. Of course, I can't be sure because I never heard a girl say so.) But you didn't talk about sex on a date. What you did was act knowing and grope around in the dark.

Did anyone dare to talk honestly? Who dared to say right out loud, "I really need some help understanding sexuality. Do you know anything? Can you help me understand this stuff?" No one dared to say that. Far from being a source of sexual help, the real girls we knew were just another frustrating part of the sexual puzzle. Perhaps Hefner's girls were not real girls.

After we got married, many of us did not talk about our sexuality. We had sexual intercourse, which we enjoyed, but in many ways there was still a cloud of confusion covering much of that important part of our lives. Most distressing of all, we still did not know where to turn for help. The doctors talked only about biological facts, the social organizations spoke only of diseases and unwanted pregnancies, and the church simply did not talk. Any thinking you did concerning sexuality, you did all alone!

Eventually, we had the sexual revolution of the sixties. Society rebelled against the old traditions and threw off its clothes. Suddenly everything was up front. The shock was almost too much for us, especially those of us who were Christians. What should we think? What should we do? Most of us probably felt some secret, inner gladness that it was OK to talk openly about sex, but it was still scary. It seemed that society was going too far. Mere nakedness and sexual conversation were not enough in themselves. If the new sexual revolution did not produce helpful insight into the meaning and nature of sexuality, including the implications of sexuality for spiritual development, we all might end up being worse off than before.

In recent years we have been inundated with literature on the general subject of sexuality. Finally, we seem to be talking. There are even books on sexuality without pictures! Even the church is talking. What a great relief to be able to read about and discuss this side of our lives that has been such a significant part of our struggle to understand ourselves.

But do you understand your sexuality? You may be very much like me—still groping along, trying to put a number of undefined questions into meaningful form, still listening hard to everything that is said in the tired hope that some answers really do exist.

Well, it may seem a bit bold of me, having just admitted that I am still only a groper after truth, to now burst into print on the subject of sexuality. So allow me to say emphatically that I do not think of myself as an authority on this subject. I am a learner, just like you. I am looking for answers, too. But I have learned some things, and it has become increasingly clear to me that these things should be shared with others. If anything that I have learned should prove helpful to you, my purpose will have been fulfilled.

2

Defining
Sexuality

T here is an ancient tale about four blind men who gathered around an elephant, felt different parts of his body, and then proceeded to describe the creature to one another. "The elephant is like a wall," declared the one who had felt the elephant's side. "No," cried the one who had felt the elephant's leg, "the elephant is like a tree." "Not at all," said the one who had felt the trunk, "the elephant is like a snake." "But it seems to me that the elephant is most like a rope," spoke the one who was holding the elephant's tail in his hand.

As we in our modern age attempt to discuss sexuality, we are somewhat similar to those ancient blind men. A great variety of explanations of the meaning of sexuality are available, most of them with some validity. But we seem to be getting only partial definitions of sexuality from the world around us. What we need most so that we can think clearly about our sexuality is a correct definition, a definition that calls attention to the whole picture and brings the parts into proper relationship to one another.

What Sexuality Is Not

Before I state what I think sexuality is, I want to mention some things it isn't. I do this just to clear the way for the definition I will later offer. It seems to me that the prevalent confusion of terms and ideas demands that we define our terms as we speak. You may not agree with my definition, but at least you will understand what I mean by use of the term *sexuality*.

No Substitute for God

First of all, sexuality is not a substitute for God; that is, it is no substitute for a personal relationship with God. Now, why would I say such a strange thing? Who in the world ever thought that sex was a substitute for God? Well, it's doubtful that anyone consciously formulated the concept that sexuality was God (although there have been cultures in which sexual activity has been thought of as a method of communion with God, and in which sexual activity was actually used as a part of the worship ceremony).

Still, many people in many societies, and certainly in ours, have approached sexuality in a manner that may be described only as worshipful. Our society in the last thirty years has grown steadily into a sex-obsessed society. Our books, movies, music, clothing styles, and a tremendous amount of media advertising consistently pound a sexual message into our brains. Underneath it all is a powerful statement of the place of sexual things in our modern view of human life.

We are being told that life aims largely, if not entirely, at sexual fulfillment. And the assumption seems to be that if we aim for it and seek it with all our hearts (not to mention our time and money), we shall soon achieve the atomic sexual experience, and presumably, we shall be fulfilled and complete. That attitude, I submit, is idolatrous.

You see, when anyone tells you that anything other than God Himself can make you fulfilled and happy, that person is encouraging you toward idolatry. Idolatry, after all, is nothing more or less than placing something other than the true and living God in first place in your life. No matter what it may be, if you place something in first place in your life, that thing has become a "god" to you, and you have become involved in a form of false worship.

When persons turn to idolatry, whatever the specific form, two things inevitably occur. First, they expect the thing worshiped (the false god) to be able to do for them what only the true and living God can do—they expect the "god" to complete and fulfill them, to give lasting meaning to their lives, and to guide them safely and serenely through life's storms. The result, of course, is always disappointment and emptiness. They have asked the "god" to supply for them what it was never designed to supply, and what it cannot supply—ultimate fulfillment or happiness. Literally millions of people in our society have swallowed the "Playboy Philosophy" only to end up disillusioned and burned out.

Second, when people turn to idolatry they lose the true meaning of the thing they have chosen as their idol. When idolators put their idol in the place of highest significance in their minds, they remove it from its proper and correct place. The result is that it is no longer able to provide the good it was designed to provide when God created it.

All things, including sexuality, were created by God with His good purpose inherent in them. God designed human sexuality for the good and for the blessing of man and woman. But that good and blessing can be obtained only by those who maintain the proper perspective on their sexuality. If we take sexuality out of its proper place, we will lose the right perspective on its meaning and use, and consequently, we will lose the blessing God means to give to us through our sexuality.

Simply put, I am saying this: sexuality must not be put in God's place. If it is, it will lose its power to bless and further human life. Sexuality, like all other created aspects of human nature, is only a part of our createdness and must, therefore, be subordinated to God, like everything else. Although sexuality is not to be worshiped, it is a marvelous and wonderful part of the way God has made us. It is His gift to us, and when it is properly understood and enjoyed, it provides us with much that is good.

Not the Same as Love

Second, our society seems to confuse sexual things with love. Indeed, sexuality, as God intends it, has something to do with love, and sexuality cannot be understood properly apart from its intrinsic involvement with love. But there are many ways to express one's sexuality that are not very loving, and there are many ways to express love that are not sexual.

An obvious example of unloving expression of sexuality is rape. Clearly, rape involves one's sexual nature; but it is just as clearly not a loving expression. Rape is a violent mistreatment of another person. Prostitution is also a sexual matter, but it is also not to be identified as a loving relationship. Prostitution is business, pure and simple. Only a very confused person would think of it as love. In addition, married people sometimes choose to use their sexuality in many selfish and, therefore, unloving ways.

Many people have experienced great confusion and pain because they have mistakenly supposed that some sexual stirring was identical to love. For instance, a woman yields to a man's sexual demands, all the while assuming that his sexual desire for her means that he loves her (perhaps she, too, assumes that she love him). But when the morning comes, the "love" vanishes with the night. The point is simply this: we must distinguish between sexual desire and love. It would be a mistake for me to assume that just because some sexual urge began to well up within me, I necessarily love the person who happens to be the object of those feelings at the moment. Or to reverse the emphasis, it is foolish to assume that just because someone expresses sexual desire toward me, that person loves me.

I know that the inability to recognize the difference between desire and love caused many problems for me when I was growing up. On more than one occasion I was convinced that I was in love with some girl I had spotted merely because she stirred some surge of genital need within me. I was having strong feelings, to be sure, but in many cases I didn't even know the girl by name. Love, one would think, should at least take the time to learn the girl's name.

It is a rather simple thing to determine if I have sexual urges in the direction of some woman, but it is a much more complicated thing to determine whether or not I have love for her. To know that I love her, I must ask myself many questions beyond whether I desire her body's pleasures. To know that I love her, I must concern myself with her whole being; I must want all of her—not just her body. To love her, I must desire her whole personality, her mind's peculiar way of thinking, her varying moods, her attitudes, and her interests.

And beyond that, if I love her, I must be willing to make certain commitments to her, not only for the moment (mere sexual urges may be quite brief, you know) but for the future as well. Recall the familiar concepts of the marriage vow: "for better or for worse," "in sickness and in health," "for richer or for poorer." Such thoughts go beyond sexual things to the whole of life. They ask the person to commit himself to his beloved in every area of life and for the duration of life. Of course, sexuality is a part of that commitment and properly understood, becomes a central part of it. But sexuality is one thing, and love is another.

I should add that other kinds of love do not include sexual expressions. I love a number of women other than my wife, but these relationships are not sexually motivated and include no sexual expressions. I love my mother, my sister, and my daughters. I hug and kiss them and enjoy their touch, but I have never felt sexual stirrings toward any of them. Indeed, if I did become sexually interested in any of them, love would require me to correct myself and abandon such thoughts or desires. I also have love for many women who are not members of my family. These are my sisters and daughters in the family of God. For them, I have deep feelings of affection, and I express that affection to them in various ways. But these relationships are not sexual in nature and should not become sexually involved. It would be irresponsible for me to become sexually motivated in these relationships. My love for them is of a different kind. It is real love, but it is not sexual.

One last distinction may prove helpful here. In love relationships there are expressions of affection. Warm handshakes, hugs, and kisses may express deep and honest love between persons. Such expressions are not necessarily sexual in nature, though. Physical touch is legitimate in its own right and may play an important role in all love relationships. But physical touch is not necessarily sexual, and neither is the desire for physical touch necessarily a sexual desire.

I think that this last distinction is significant for a variety of reasons. Many people in our society (and particularly in the church) carry around a burden of false guilt because they are affectionate persons who enjoy touch. In our society "touchy" persons are sometimes wrongly viewed as being sexually intentioned. Therefore, if I, a man, reach out to touch a woman affectionately, I may be interpreted as sending her a sexual overture. Or if I affectionately touch another man, I may be viewed as having homosexual tendencies.

This kind of thing has had damaging effects on men in our society. Many men have grown very wary of touching anyone, especially other men, because of their mistaken assumption that all touch must, of necessity, be sexual. Touch in itself is merely physical. Even when it is genuinely loving touch and expressive of deep emotion, it still is not necessarily sexual, for one may genuinely love apart from sexual motivation.

Much more needs to be said about the nature of love, and subsequent chapters address that topic. What is the difference between being "in love" and truly loving someone? How can one know when a loving relationship is about to become sexual? Or how can one know that feelings are entirely sexual and not at all loving? All these and other questions need careful answers, and they will be given consideration later in this book.

Right now we are searching for a definition of sexuality, and it is enough to say that we must look further than the general matter of the ability to love. Love is much broader and more all-encompassing than sexuality. Love has to do with how one chooses to treat another person. It has to do with decisions about what is truly good for another person, and what would be responsible and useful for me to give that person. It has to do with commitments and promises. Sexuality, on the other hand, is a part of my nature. I may choose to do loving things with my sexuality, or I may choose to do selfish and unloving things with it. We must look further for our definition.

Not Just Biological Sex

A third way in which we may be confused about sexuality is in our tendency to identify it only with biological sex. We may understandably make such a mistake in a culture like ours. The prevailing spirit of modern-day society toward sex seems to be that it is physical and nothing more. Therefore, we may easily think that sexuality involves only what two people are able to do with their bodies to create pleasure.

If you walk into bookstores and browse among the many offerings on the subject of sexuality, you will quickly see that they focus on how to achieve maximum physical pleasure. Most books deal with "how to" have sexual intercourse. Their subject is the method of "doing" sex. They offer suggestions on what to touch and when to touch it to produce the greatest amount of physical pleasure possible. By and large, these books define sexuality as merely physical, and they tell us by implication that the purpose of sexual relationships goes no further than the physical. They make no comment about the responsibilities of the two people engaging in sexual relationships. There is no talk about meaning or morality. There is no guidance for making sexual choices. They are "mechanics illustrated" books for sex partners. No wonder we tend to believe that sexuality is nothing more than something our bodies do.

But sexuality is far more. There is the whole matter of what goes on inside our heads and hearts when we bring our bodies so close together. Sexuality has to do with what my sex partner and I are thinking and desiring and meaning. Sexuality has to do with my purpose and my partner's purpose and our ability to communicate and discuss and understand our purposes. Sexuality, you see, is far more than physical. It is intensely personal and spiritual, and I think that deep inside we all know that this is true.

Sexuality Is Spiritual

It may sound strange to say that sexuality is spiritual, but it really does not take much to prove it. If you have any degree of sexual experience, you know already that mere biological sex can easily be very frustrating and empty. It is quite possible to have intercourse, even to the point of vibrant orgasm, without having much personal, inner satisfaction. Many married people feel negatively about their physical sexual relationship, and I believe the greatest reason is that the spiritual aspect of their sexuality is being ignored.

A compelling proof of what I am saying is the widespread occurrence of sexual affairs among married persons. What are those straying spouses looking for? Is it mere physical sex? Sometimes, perhaps. Generally, their stories tell of the desire for a personal relationship of quality. Something far more significant than mere physical sexual satisfaction was missing in their marriages. Usually, they report that they felt lonely, unattractive, and unimportant in their relationship with their spouse. In many cases they will even say that the physical side of their marriage was pretty good, but "something" was lacking. That "something" is almost always of a spiritual nature.

In his remarkable movie *Annie Hall* Woody Allen makes this point very forcefully. There is a scene in which Woody and his costar, Diane Keaton, are in bed together preparing to have intercourse. Diane is not able to relax, and Woody senses that something is wrong. She denies it and urges him to just go on with things.

Then a very strange thing happens to Diane. She seems to divide in half; that is, suddenly there are two Dianes. While Diane and Woody continue to lie in bed, a second Diane, a ghostly, see-through Diane, appears, gets out of the bed, steps across the room, sits in a chair, and stares back at the two in bed. The look on her face shows plainly that she is bored.

Then she speaks, "Alvie [this is Woody's character], do you remember where I put my drawing pad? Because while you two are doing that, I think I'm going to do some drawing."

Alvie seems a bit distressed by this turn of events and replies with irritation, "You see, that's what I call removed."

Now she is upset, but answers as if there is really no problem, "No, come on, you have my body."

Now Alvie seems hurt. "But that's not—look, I want the whole thing," he says.

At first it seems to be a very funny scene. Everyone in the movie house chuckles. Ha, ha, ha. But it is funny only a moment. By the time the scene is over no one is laughing. It is funny only on the surface. Deep down inside we all know from experience the loneliness, hurt, and anger that sometime accompany sexual intercourse. A man and a woman may unite physically and yet feel very far from each other in personal and spiritual ways.

Look a little more closely at what Woody and Diane are saying to each other in the movie. Diane is hurt and angry because she feels that all Woody really wants from her is the use of her body to satisfy his physical pleasure. Woody, however, seems hurt, too. He is hurt because all Diane will give him is her body. He wants her spirit, too. The moment she withdraws her spirit from him he notices, and he is hurt. He wants "the whole thing." Both Woody and Diane know that sexuality involves "the whole thing."

I think the saddest part about that scene from *Annie Hall* is that you know while you are watching it, those two people are not really communicating. They are in bed together. They are having intercourse, but within themselves they are hurting. They are unhappy with what they are doing. They wish it was better; they long for it to be better. They are physically together, but they feel miles apart spiritually. The whole episode is not just a cinematic creation. Life can be this way. Woody Allen has identified something most people have experienced, and in so doing he has provided some real help in defining sexuality.

Our sexuality longs for more than mere physical union. We may feel driven by physical needs, and intercourse may relieve the tensions for a moment. But that is not all we want. We want personal and spiritual union. We want belonging. We want interest and care. We want faithfulness and trust and the assurance and peace that those bring. Any definition of sexuality that excludes these things is only a partial and inadequate definition.

Let us then attempt a definition of this thing we call sexuality. Sexuality is the human potential for the complete sharing of one's whole life with another. It is the potential for sharing on both spiritual and physical levels in a whole-life and lifelong union. It is the ability and the need imprinted upon one's nature by the Creator to give oneself completely to another human being. It is also the ability and the need to receive another person into one's life in a total and complete way. Perhaps the old romantic expression "body and soul" says it best. I have the ability and the need to give myself, all of myself, the body and soul of myself, to another person.

I have the ability and the need to receive another, all of another, the body and soul of another into my life. As a sexual being, I have the potential for union that includes my whole being and the whole being of another.[1]

1. I am deeply indebted to the work of Lewis Smedes in his book *Sex for Christians* (Grand Rapids: William B. Eerdmans, 1976) for his thorough and comprehensive study of the meaning of sexuality. Anyone interested in further study of the nature and meaning of sexuality should take the time to read this book.

3

The Meaning of Sexual Intercourse

T hey had a party at Max Yasgur's place over twenty years ago, and we're still cleaning up the mess. It was the weekend of August 15–17, 1969, when 400,000 youths gathered on Mr. Yasgur's dairy farm in the little Catskill town of Bethel, on White Lake, about seventy miles northwest of New York City for a festival of rock music. They called it Woodstock because it had originally been planned for the Hudson River village by that name. The name stuck and soon became a name full of symbolism for the whole society. Woodstock, more than any other single event of the sixties, created a new sense of identity for the young. It also revealed to members of the older generation how wide the gap between them and their children had become.

Much about Woodstock stunned the watching American society. Just the size of the whole thing was staggering. It was also remarkably well organized. The kids were peaceful and courteous, so much so that a police officer commented that in all his years in law enforcement, he had never seen such a considerate and well-behaved bunch. They had, in one sense, gotten together to celebrate peace and love. They wanted an end to the fighting in Vietnam. They believed in world brotherhood, and while their favorite bands sang about peace, they held hands in symbolic union.

But hands were not all that they united. Perhaps the most shocking thing to the parents who heard the reports of Woodstock and later saw the film that was produced was the wide-open sexual freedom of many attendees. They took off their clothes, and many of them copulated in the daylight in full view. One reporter told of seeing a nude couple, apparently strangers, who approached each other, lay in the grass for a while in sexual embrace, then moved on their separate ways. They never spoke.

The sexual freedom of Woodstock was hailed by the voices of the young as a symbol of new freedom from outworn social mores. Many older persons probably wished they were still young. Whatever it all meant, Bob Dylan's song spoke the truth—"the times they are a'changin'." Indeed, the times had already changed, and Woodstock was amazing evidence of the extent of that change.

Of all the changes, none is more obvious than our apparent decision that sexual intercourse has no inherent meaning. If two strangers who bump into each other quite by accident happen to choose a genital greeting rather than the spoken word or a handshake, what difference does it make anyway? Can we argue against such a thing between consenting adults? Must we attach so much significance to sexual intercourse? Is it not just a way of being friendly after all? And what could be friendlier?

The American attitude frequently seems to be that sexual intercourse does not have any meaning except the meaning two consenting people choose to give it. These days we hear that the older views asserting that intercourse meant "love" or "commitment" or at least deep passion are not necessarily true. Intercourse seems to be neutral. It may mean love if two people choose that it means love. It may mean excitement for one night only if that is what two people choose for it to mean. But in the end no rules universally apply regarding intercourse. Whatever turns you on— and whatever you feel comfortable with—is now acceptable.

What Are You Comfortable With?

But comfort is not as easily achieved as we might like to think. Despite all our public protesting that sexual intercourse is only a highly pleasing diversion, we have a hard time not believing that it has meaning. In spite of ourselves we seem to think that it means far more than entertainment. We may talk as if it is perfectly acceptable for two consenting adults to share a little of their genitals with whomever they please and for whatever reason seems pleasing, but our attitudes usually change when one of those consenting adults is close to us. We will not rest very well if the adult who casually sleeps around happens to be our own baby sister or our middle-aged mother. In those cases we will start to think of what is "proper" or even "moral."

Neither is it a simple thing to find comfort in regard to our personal sexual behavior. Counselors' offices are filled today with people who thought they were liberated from the old idea of the "meaning" of sexual intercourse, but they have discovered after a while that intercourse has a way of bringing meaning along for the ride.

In the movie *10* Dudley Moore plays a frustrated forty-year-old who fears that life's joys may be passing him by, and he becomes desperately infatuated with a beautiful woman (Bo Derek) much younger than himself. He follows her on her honeymoon, and through a series of most unlikely events, he manages to rescue her husband from death. While the husband is in the hospital, Dudley goes to the wife's hotel room and discovers that she is wonderfully open to a sexual relationship with him. Every man's wildest sexual fantasy now has become his. What fun!

Then something happens to spoil the fun. At the very moment that they are beginning to have intercourse, the husband calls. Dudley is stunned when the wife then acknowledges to her husband that he is there with her and even hands the phone to him so that he may speak with her husband. After the phone is hung up, we discover that Dudley is hung up, too.

How could she tell her husband that he was there? What would her husband think if he knew what she was doing? She replies that her husband wouldn't mind at all because what she does is her business, and further-more she wouldn't mind if her husband wanted to sleep with others. That would be his business. Well then, Dudley would like to know, what exactly is the meaning (there's that word) of her being in bed with him?

At this point Dudley says, "I would like to think that I'm more than a casual lay."

His balloon is popped when she replies, "Whatever made you think you were anything else?"

Dudley is devastated. It is in fact only a casual lay. He does not know the woman. He has not been drawn to her by any personal knowledge of what she is really like. He knows only that she is beautiful, and he has imagined that sexual intercourse with her would be a wonderful experi-ence. He discovers to his surprise that he is motivated by a desire for more than a physical sexual massage. He does not want this to be casual. He wants it to have meaning. At least he wants to imagine that it has meaning. He does not want the woman to be so matter-of-fact in saying that it is only casual.

There is keen commentary on our sexual nature here. We are usually not able to be happy with what is called casual sex. One wonders if there can be such a thing at all. Perhaps on the surface we can act as if we do not need the deeper, inner meaning of sexual intercourse. But it is not very easy to just have intercourse with our bodies. Somehow our bodies seem to be inextricably connected to our souls. And our souls demand interpretation of our actions in meaningful terms. As we watch the movie *10,* we end up finding Dudley Moore more believable than Bo Derek.

Our natures seem to give us a message about our sexuality. It is both spirit and body, and we cannot separate the two. We have intercourse with our spirits as well as our bodies. As Lewis Smedes says, we cannot take our bodies to bed with someone and park our souls outside in the car to wait.[1] We may try to do so, but in the end it is impossible.

I remember counseling a married woman who had had an affair. She was very cold and unemotional as she told me about it. It had not meant anything at all, she declared. She had been silly to do such a thing. And after all, she said, "All I gave him was my body."

In the conversation that followed, I pressed her to back up such a statement. Eventually she was in tears as she admitted that her soul had been very much present during intercourse with the man. She had hoped that he would love her, wanted him to care about her in a lasting way, wanted him to share her heart. It had proved to be a relationship without a future, and her heart was filled with disappointment, guilt, and shame. How could she feel those things if all she had given him was her body? In reality she had given him more. It is impossible to have intercourse and bring only one's body to bed. It is impossible because of the way we were made by our Creator.

The Symbolism of Intercourse

Christians have always affirmed that the only way to discover truth is to listen to what God has said. The way to find the meaning of sexual intercourse, therefore, is not to heed the latest survey of the opinions of Americans. Neither can we simply look into our personal feelings on the matter. We must listen to God the Creator. He has made us sexual creatures, and He alone can give us clear understanding of the meaning of sexual intercourse.

The meaning God has given to sexual intercourse is that of the marriage union. Sexual intercourse is symbolic of the whole-life sharing that God requires of spouses. God invented it to be such a symbol and, in fact, a seal of that union. It was not given to mankind merely for physical pleasure; rather, it was given to indicate in an outward way what has happened and is happening in the souls of the two people who so unite.

Think about how the act of sexual intercourse actually illustrates the spiritual union of married love. In intercourse one person, the man, literally enters the body of the other, the woman. There is in that entrance a symbol of what ought to be happening in his spirit at the same time. He ought to be saying to her, "I am willing to enter into your life, into your whole life. I want to come into who and what you are. I want to discover you in every way. As I discover you, I will love you and accept you. I will not reject what I find that you are. I will care for you, understand you, and always honor you. I will dwell lovingly within your life."

On the other side of the illustration, think of the symbolism of the woman's act of intercourse. She actually opens her body to the man's entrance. She ought to be saying, "You may come into my whole life. I will keep no secrets from you. What I truly am I will permit you to know, to touch. I will trust you wholly with my inner self. You are welcome here inside my life."

Here is the meaning of sexual intercourse: two people are given to each other in whole-life sharing; they mutually give and receive of themselves. That is the reason traditional Christian morality has always insisted the only persons who should have the privilege of sexual intercourse are those who marry. Intercourse stands as an outward, bodily symbol of the pledged love of the marriage union.

It is, therefore, a sinful thing to have sexual intercourse outside marriage. It is sinful because it violates the inherent meaning of sexual intercourse and the very humanity of the two persons who commit the act. People who decide to have sexual intercourse without also having mutual commitment to whole-life (and lifelong) sharing actually decide against their own wholeness and happiness. When people choose to sin, they choose to bring pain upon themselves.

You just can't separate sexuality into parts without creating pain. When people seek to enjoy the physical pleasures of sexuality without the spiritual pleasures, they will find in time that the physical sexual experience becomes empty and hurtful.

I once spoke with a former prostitute who had become a Christian. I asked her to describe what it had been like to live as she had. She said that at first it felt like a marvelous trip. Every man thought she was beautiful. Many told her of her desirability. When she had pangs of conscience, she told herself that she was just remembering her old-fashioned upbringing, that she was a "liberated" woman, that these were modern times.

Eventually, however, she realized that she was just a commodity for sale, that the men she sold herself to had no personal interest in her and no respect. She recognized that she was losing her ability to place any value on the act of sexual intercourse, and she was having difficulty knowing if she believed in such a thing as love. She lacked self-esteem and gained a deep distrust of men. Her activity brought her no spiritual pleasures.

What do I mean by the "spiritual pleasures" of sexuality? I mean the pleasures accompanying the knowledge that I am loved honestly and certainly. I am talking about the assurance that my sexual partner is not only enjoying my body at the moment, but is devoted to me—and me alone. I am talking about the certainty that my sexual partner loves me as a whole person, and not merely for what my body is able to do for her.

The spiritual pleasures of sexuality also include the joy and delight of knowing that I am loved regardless of how well I perform in physical sex on a given day or that I am loved as well on a day when there is no intercourse at all. There are, after all, more days in a marriage without sexual intercourse than there are days with it. One of the greatest spiritual pleasures of married sexuality is the knowledge that one does not have to perform as if he just got off the boat from Paris in order to be sexually fulfilled or loved.

For happily married persons, sexual intercourse is no longer on center stage. No matter how passionately they may feel the need for each other physically before they marry and during the first months of marriage, all married people sooner or later settle down into a much more relaxed and quiet pace physically.

They still enjoy physical sex, but it is not the demanding, urgent matter it once was. It seems to have found its proper place as the icing on the cake of their committed love. They may have thought that it was the cake, but they have learned that their love is a spiritual matter and that sexual intercourse is only one of many ways to express their love. A powerful and delightful way, no doubt, but not the only way or even the most important way.

These fortunate persons understand that the relationship they share within their spirits is far more powerful and meaningful than anything they can do with their bodies. When they love each other by means of sexual intercourse, they understand it as a celebration of their lasting love based on far more than the ability to create erotic pleasure. It is based on the knowledge of a promise that they have made to each other, the promise to love each other faithfully through all the varieties of life's experience, no matter what changes may come. Only the marriage promise can create such pleasure.

The Importance of Commitment

Many individuals argue against the necessity for the marriage commitment. Two people can enjoy the pleasures of sexuality without marriage, they say. They argue this in two ways. First, they declare that it is possible to separate the two aspects of sexuality. One can enjoy the physical, genital, erotic pleasures of sexuality without possessing the spiritual and personal assurances. Of course, in a sense they are right!

I am not saying that the physical pleasures are not possible apart from the spiritual assurances. But I am saying that where those spiritual and personal commitments do not exist, there cannot be the fullness and total satisfaction our sexuality yearns for. Beyond that, I am also saying that those who have intercourse outside the marriage bond guarantee for themselves the experience of inward spiritual pain in one form or another.

The spiritual pain that can accompany sexual intercourse for the unmarried includes fear, guilt, and loneliness. All of these negatives grow directly out of the absence of the mutual commitment to whole-life sharing and support given in the marriage vows. The woman (or man) who wonders, "Will he (she) still respect me in the morning?" is inwardly voicing the fear that she (he) is not being loved honestly and certainly.

We are often told that the guilt sometimes accompanying sexual intercourse between unmarried persons has been created by our social or religious upbringing. But its true cause is much deeper and much more personal. Each of us knows instinctively that love, to be real, must be committed love! We also know that if we have had intercourse with someone to whom we are not married, we have given something less than that. We have not given our whole selves to each other, and we know instinctively that we should.

Persons who manage to avoid the fear and guilt (and I sincerely doubt that they really exist) will never be able to escape the loneliness. The more individuals insist on physical sexual pleasure without the undergirding of personal commitments of love, the more they build an insurmountable wall around themselves. The loneliness (the deep, inner desire for soul sharing) will grow greater with each new experience. Loneliness is solved only by the sharing of hearts, not bodies. A great tragedy of our day is the acceptance of "new" folk wisdom asserting that intimacy can be created by bringing our bodies together. It doesn't work, and those who believe it does will try it again and again only to end up disillusioned and alone.

Yes, people may enjoy the physical pleasures of sexuality apart from the spiritual pleasures, but they can never do so without denying some very basic needs of their humanity. Everyone needs the joy and satisfaction of committed love. The longer people tell themselves that they don't, the more inner distress they will create for themselves by continuing to have intercourse outside marriage.

The second way in which people attempt to argue against the necessity of the marriage commitment is by making personal commitments to each other short of marriage that provide a kind of safeguard around their sexual involvement. The common practice of living together is the prime example of this approach. Of course, arrangements of living together do not prove that commitment is unnecessary. In fact, they prove quite the opposite! The couple who live together are saying by their decision that a certain commitment exists. Although they do not take the final step of formal marriage, they demonstrate that they know sexuality is more than a merely physical involvement. All they lack is the willingness to make a public commitment that would bind them together legally in a marriage recognized and honored in society.

In the final consideration, however, the couple who live together fail to give each other the ultimate assurance of committed love. At any time, one or the other could simply get up and move out. Nothing binds them on a permanent, whole-life basis. "Will you still respect me in the morning?" has merely been extended to "Will you still respect me in six months or a year?"

Marriage, and marriage alone, provides the solid foundation and framework necessary for the full expression of one's sexuality. I must emphasize that I am speaking of marriage in the historic Christian sense of a permanent whole-life commitment between two persons. That's right—till death do us part! Nothing else but that absolute promise will do the job. Any other view of marriage is susceptible to the same weakness that living together is. If our view of marriage is that it is valid and binding only until the point that one party decides to get up and leave it behind, we do not have what our sexuality cries out for most deeply. We do not have committed love.

Some people will argue against marriage precisely on the ground that I have just given. How can anyone possibly know oneself or one's spouse-to-be well enough to make a permanent lifelong commitment such as that? No one can know what will happen in the future. People change. This is the spirit of our age, which asks how a commitment can be made when we all know full well that things change.

My answer is that you cannot know for sure unless you commit for sure. Marriage cannot possibly be safe for anyone if it is based on things that change. It must be based on something that will never change. That is why the vow of commitment is so significant. Marriage, to be safe, must be based on unconditional promises of love. The marriage vow says, "I will love you even if you do change." It goes further than that and says, "I will love you even if I change." Only the people who are willing to make that commitment to each other and to become that vulnerable to each other have the right to the delights of sexual intercourse, because that is what sexual intercourse symbolizes. Without the inner commitment of love made certain by promise, sexual intercourse becomes a mere momentary physical pleasure.

1. Smedes, *Sex for Christians,* p. 132.

CHAPTER 4

Coming Back to Single Life

A few years ago I was speaking at a Fresh Start Seminar* on the subject of single sexuality. I had just finished giving my definition of the meaning of sexual intercourse, much as I have done in the previous chapter. Suddenly a woman in the crowd got up and walked out. She was plainly upset. When my talk was finished, I sought her out and asked to talk with her.

"What you were saying up there is exactly what I always thought I believed," she told me through tears. "I grew up in a Christian home. We always read the Bible and prayed together. I never questioned the nature of sexuality or marriage. I always believed that God had created sex for marriage only. I was still a virgin when I married.

"For fifteen years I thought we were very happily married," she continued. "Then David just seemed to drift away from me. He started working late and on weekends. When he did come home, he never talked. He seldom wanted to go out or take a trip with me. His interest in sex lessened. Then last spring he just announced that he wanted out. He was in love with someone else."

I asked her what it was about my presentation that had so upset her.

---

*Fresh Start Seminars, Inc., is a help seminar for divorced and separated persons that originated in 1980 at the Church of the Saviour in Wayne, Pennsylvania. Since that time Fresh Start has grown into a ministry that offers weekend seminars to churches through the eastern and southern parts of the country. For information about Fresh Start write: Fresh Start Seminars, Inc., 651 N. Wayne Avenue, Wayne, PA 19087.

"It was when you started talking about commitment," she replied. "I feel like I made that very commitment. That was what I believed, and that was what I lived all those years. Now look what it got me. He's off having a great time with his new wife, and I'm alone trying to survive."

"But do you think that I was wrong to teach the importance of commitment?" I questioned. "Do you no longer believe in the need for commitment if a marriage is going to work?"

"I really don't know what I believe anymore," she said. "It all sounds so nice and Christian, but I just don't know if it's really worth it to trust anybody that much again. Maybe all these people are right who are telling us to live for ourselves and whatever passing pleasures we can find. I just don't know."

This woman is not an isolated case. She represents the majority of people who come to our seminars. They are shocked, hurt, and confused. They have lived according to a set of beliefs and values that seems to have let them down. They feel rejected and alone. And they are bitter. The ones who are professing Christians often feel that God Himself has let them down. Sometimes they question whether they want to go on living the Christian life.

There is probably no single area in which divorced persons are driven to greater questioning of their values and beliefs than the area of sexuality. Divorced people struggle with a sense of rejection and loss of worth. They need the comfort of being loved. They need the normal enjoyment of companionship. They also need the reassurance of physical touch. Each of these normal and natural needs raises questions of a sexual nature.

Christians face additional questions related to their spiritual and moral understanding of their sexuality. And they are probably subjected to various pressures by well-meaning Christian friends or by the organized church itself. Often divorced persons discover that the church and their Christian friends are entirely unable to understand the nature of their struggle. Instead of being truly supportive, such people have frequently made it even more difficult for their divorced friends to emerge victorious from their struggle.

Rejection and Self-Worth

A devastating aspect of the divorce experience is the sense of rejection, especially for those who have not chosen to be divorced. But it is true also for the ones who have taken the active steps leading to the divorce. As I have listened to such people tell their stories, I have grown familiar with the patterns.

"Tom, I tried. I really did. I tried with all my heart. I did everything that she asked me to do. Again and again I could see that she was unhappy. I would ask her what she wanted. How could I help? Was I doing something wrong? I would have done anything in my power to please her."

His name was Bill, and he was the picture of helplessness and despair as he poured out his tale of frustrated attempts to improve his relationship with his former wife. After he had talked a long time and seemed exhausted by reliving the pain, I asked, "Did she ever say anything to indicate some complaint against you? Surely she told you something."

"Finally, she did," he answered. "It was the day she was leaving the house. Everything was packed. The children were sitting in the car. I had kissed them good-bye. Then we walked around the car to the driver's side. She looked at me and said, 'I'm sorry it has to be like this.' I said, 'If only I knew what I did wrong.'" He dropped his head and sighed.

"What did she say?" I asked.

He continued, "She told me it really wasn't anything that I had done. She said that she knew I had tried. It was just that I didn't have what it took to make her happy." He choked up, and his eyes filled with tears.

What a blow that must have been! What could be more defeating than to hear your mate tell you that she knew you had done your best, but that it just wasn't good enough? It would be far easier to be told about your faults. Maybe then you could learn from failure. But if you did your best and that still wasn't good enough, well, maybe you just aren't any good at all.

I happened to know Bill's wife. I had counseled with her also. She had come from a terribly dysfunctional family. She had married Bill when she was eighteen, largely motivated by the need to escape her parents. She had struggled with self-esteem all her life. In my judgment, she did not know how to be happy with herself. I sincerely doubted that there was a man alive who could have done any better at loving her than Bill had done. And I told him so. But he was a defeated man, and my encouragement was little help.

Bill's sense of rejection and accompanying self-doubt created inner questions about his value as a person. He began to believe that he really was not very likable. For a while he continued to see old friends and to remain active in his church. But soon it seemed to him that he was taking all the initiative with his friends. He was not asked to participate in social events as much as before. At church he felt that he was something of an embarrassment. Finally, he left the church and drifted away from his old friends.

A great void was opening up inside Bill that had far-reaching sexual implications. At first he retreated into himself. Another woman in his life was the farthest thing from his mind. He could not see himself as desirable or interesting; he was threatened by the thought of a relationship with a woman. He had failed once, and once was enough, he thought. He told me, "There is no possibility of another woman getting that close to my heart. I will never allow myself to become that vulnerable again."

In six months Bill was in love again. Judy was a wonderful woman who worked in the office with Bill. He had known her casually for a long time and respected her. Even though she had been divorced several years, she had never dated. She worked hard raising her children and kept to herself. She, like Bill, was a sincere Christian. One day at work she had to talk with him about a project they were both working on. She paused to ask him if he was doing all right. He bravely replied that he was fine. Then she made a remark that would touch Bill's deepest needs.

"I think you are such a fine man," she said, "and sometimes my heart just hurts for you."

Bill told me that Judy's statement had meant a lot to him. It just felt good to have a woman like her say such a positive thing to him. If someone like Judy thought he was a fine man, well, maybe he really wasn't such a bad guy after all. We talked about the possible implications of his rising sense of self-worth. I asked him if he thought that Judy was attracted to him. He said he didn't think so. I asked him if he was attracted to her. He said that she was a nice lady, but no, not really. As Bill left my office, I thought to myself, *The guy's a dead duck.*

What happened next is a long and unhappy story. I will say only that after a brief but torrid love affair, Bill discovered that he was incapable of growing in love for Judy. She was much stronger than he was and was ready for a growing relationship of trust and mutual dependency. She expected him to be able to grow in those ways with her, but he could not. The result was a breakup and wounded feelings on both sides.

The point of the story is that Bill's experience of rejection and subsequent sense of worthlessness had so crippled him emotionally that he had become incapable of a meaningful sexual experience. He and Judy had been sleeping together, and for a time, it seemed to them that the earth had stopped moving. All the love songs were written just for them, and they lived in a fantasy world of beauty and wonder. It was what he had always known love should be. They talked about everything, and they seemed to understand each other so well.

But something inside Bill was broken. His divorce experience had shattered his sense of self-worth. He had come to doubt that he was capable of providing what a woman needs in a relationship. Certainly the doubt was not fully apparent on the surface of Bill's life. It was not even something Bill understood at first, or he would not have entered into the relationship with Judy. It was there nonetheless, buried in his inmost soul. As Judy's understanding and affection touched him more and more deeply, Bill grew more and more restless and frightened. Finally, to protect himself from what he was feeling, Bill simply had to create the safety of distance from Judy.

Bill's story illustrates the spiritual dimension of our sexuality. If a sexual relationship were only a physical matter, Bill would have had no problems at all. The physical relationship he had with Judy was apparently very exciting and pleasurable. The power of those times with her was so great that for a while he was able to ignore his deeper needs. But soon Bill found himself dealing with more than bodily pleasures.

As Bill and Judy had become more and more involved with physical sex, the deeper, spiritual realities of their sexual nature had come to the surface. The questions of the meaning (remember that word?) of outward, physical activity had to be answered. At that point the extent of Bill's woundedness became clearer. His rejection and the resultant loss of self-worth had crippled him so seriously that he was unable to provide his physical sexual activity with the spiritual undergirding it needed.

He cared very much about Judy. He respected her as a person. He saw only the best qualities in her. He wanted only good things for her. More than that, he felt he needed her. He wanted her companionship. He desired her. In many ways he thought he wanted to marry her. Yet he could not give her the deeper things that they both knew would be required if they were to have a successful marriage. In the end Bill recognized that he did not trust Judy and that he was unable to make a commitment to her.

When Bill's relationship with Judy ended, he had to deal with the new problem of guilt. The guilt took two forms. First, he knew he had compromised his moral standard. Bill was a Christian who had always believed that sexual intercourse outside marriage was sinful. He had to face the fact that he had failed the test of personal integrity. He was not the man he had believed himself to be. Second, he had injured Judy. His moral weakness had permitted him to say things to her and do things with her that, in the end, had only set her up for a fall. Bill was even more crippled than before.

Aloneness and Sexual Need

Jim and Debbie had been married eight years when Jim walked out on her and left their community. They had no children, but Debbie had her church family. Most of their old friends at church seemed very sympathetic and supportive of her. For a while they included her in most of their group activities. Some of their closest friends invited her for dinner. Gradually their attention seemed to diminish, however, and Debbie was often alone.

Debbie's very closest friends in the church were Stu and Mary. As she found herself having fewer friends, Debbie depended more on Stu and Mary. When she and Jim were together, the four of them had always been very affectionate with one another. After her divorce from Jim, Debbie observed no change in Stu and Mary for several months. They would hug her tightly and treat her as they always had. Then things changed.

One evening Debbie was at Stu and Mary's home helping them prepare dinner. At one point Debbie and Stu were in the kitchen alone working side by side. Inadvertently Stu touched Debbie's hand. A rush of confused feelings ran through her at that moment, and she pulled away from him. For the rest of the evening Debbie felt awkward, so she excused herself early. At home she pondered the meaning of what had happened.

Debbie knew that Stu had not meant to make an advance toward her. She also knew that she was not having romantic fantasies for him. Stu was like her brother. Finally she decided that she was just lonely and that she missed being touched very much. When Stu had touched her, that was what she had felt. For a moment it had just confused her. Still, she knew she had acted strangely and believed that she should explain herself to Stu and Mary. Later, at their home, Debbie explained her confusion of the previous evening and asked them to forgive her for acting so oddly.

At that point Debbie received a terrific shock. Stu and Mary had talked about their relationship with Debbie quite a lot recently, they told her. They had wondered if perhaps they were too close to her for her good. Possibly she was too dependent on them. Now it seemed that maybe she was beginning to have confused motives in her relationship with Stu. Perhaps it would be best if they did not see each other as much.

Debbie was numb. For a while she tried bravely to remain in touch with Stu and Mary, but things were never the same. Mary would still hug her, but Stu never did. She soon believed that she had become a threat to Mary and that their relationship could never be close again.

After struggling for some time, Debbie called the pastor to talk about her feelings. The pastor turned out to be less than helpful. From Debbie's point of view, he sided entirely with Stu and Mary. "These triangles always seem to develop," he said.

Triangle? Debbie could not believe what she had heard. She protested that she had never had the slightest interest in Stu, and that nothing improper had ever occurred between them. In reply the pastor gave her a brief lecture on the subtleties of the lusts of human flesh and told her that she really could not trust herself now that her sexual needs were not being met. In his opinion, the pastor told her, she should just be reconciled to the fact that she could not have close friendships with couples anymore. Debbie left feeling that she had been condemned and entirely misunderstood.

The hurt that Debbie felt made it hard for her to go to church. She could not listen to the pastor talk about love and compassion without remembering how harsh and unsympathetic he had seemed that afternoon when he talked with her. Eventually she felt that she should leave the church. But before she did, Debbie sought out John Carson. John was a retired elder in the church, a man much respected for his wisdom and kindliness.

As she talked with John Carson, Debbie felt understood.

"I believe you, Debbie," John told her. "I don't think you had any evil thoughts about Stu that night. I also believe that your strange feelings when he touched you were entirely natural and innocent."

Debbie then asked, "Mr. Carson, what should I do? I really want to straighten things out."

"I doubt if they can be straightened out," he replied. "These things are so confusing and difficult."

"Then what can I do?" she asked.

"Oh, you probably do need to leave the church and just start over somewhere," he said. "That would be the best thing for you and everyone else."

Debbie left the church, but she did not look for another one. She felt she had been let down, even betrayed, by the best friends she had. By God's people! She felt entirely alone.

Over the next two years Debbie's loneliness grew. She did not go to church, but she tried to continue living the Christian life. She read the Scriptures and listened to Christian radio programs for nurture. She prayed and tried to fellowship with God. But the Scriptural emphasis seemed to be on the importance of deep and loving friendships with others, which only intensified her growing need for companionship.

After two years Debbie met Frank. Frank was not a Christian, but he was the most tender and most understanding man she had ever met. He touched Debbie's inner heart with a caring and considerate spirit that gradually brought her out of her isolated life into a sense of wholeness. In time she knew that she loved Frank deeply. He asked her to marry him, and she said yes.

There was one problem. Debbie still thought of herself as a Christian, and she knew the Bible taught that she could not marry an unbeliever. She told Frank that she wanted to marry him, but she wanted him to know the Savior. He agreed to go to her former pastor to discuss the questions he had about Christianity.

Once again the pastor proved unhelpful. Instead of leading Frank into an encounter with Jesus Christ, the pastor only stressed that Debbie could not marry him. Frank felt that he was being told that he was not good enough for Debbie and left angrily. Later, the pastor called Debbie (after not having spoken to her in two years) and implied that she had fallen away from the Lord. He then informed her that she had been dropped from the rolls of the church.

When I met Debbie and Frank, they were searching for a minister to marry them. They had picked my name at random from the phone book. They told me that they had never been in bed together. Debbie had explained to Frank from the first that she believed she should not be sexually active unless she was married, and Frank had shown her great respect in honoring her belief. I also found Frank quite open to the claims of Christ, largely because of Debbie's moral character. Soon he had made his own profession of faith. Today they are serving the Lord together.

Debbie's story has a happy ending, and that is part of my reason for telling it. But it might have ended tragically. The stories of the lonely ordinarily do. Much of the reason for that has to do with the deep connection between loneliness and sexual need.

What does our sexual nature most long for? It is the deep, spiritual sharing of souls that Debbie eventually found with Frank. Debbie's search was for a friend, for someone with whom she could share her life. It was a search for understanding, for communion, for support, for touch. These are the things for which we all search as sexual creatures, but in that search there are many sexual pitfalls.

That Debbie was able to find the solution to her loneliness without ending up in bed with Frank marks her as the exception to the rule. In our society with its high-powered sexual style, great numbers of the lonely become convinced that the solution to their loneliness is to be found in the bedroom. Loneliness, far more than glandular excitement, drives people into bed with total strangers. Without the deep conviction of her faith Debbie could easily have substituted mere physical sex for spiritual sharing.

When I think of Debbie, my heart is full of compassion. She fought and won a battle against great odds. And sadly, the entire situation was made more difficult for her by the inability of her Christian friends and her church to understand the true nature of her struggle. From the very beginning she wanted to walk faithfully with the Lord. She was determined not to commit sexual sin, and I believe that she did not. Her friends, however, suspected her and shunned her. Their behavior only intensified her loneliness and drove her to look for support in dangerous places. I praise God for protecting her. I have met many people who were not so fortunate.

Bitterness and Relationships

Sharon's husband, Pete, was a liar, and he was a good one. He had lied to her before they got married and continued to do so as long as they were married. They had been married over ten years before she realized how serious the problem really was.

They were attending a party sponsored by Pete's company when Pete introduced her to a couple from out of town. "This is a just a gag," he whispered in her ear just before he introduced her as "my good friend, Sharon."

She was so shocked that she couldn't think of anything to say at the time. On the way home, she asked him, "Exactly what was that 'good friend' business at the party?"

"Oh, nothing, really," he replied. "Those people don't know that I'm married."

"What?" she nearly shrieked. "What are you saying?"

"It's really nothing, Sharon," he insisted. "It's just a joke some of the guys were playing, and I went along with it. It's really nothing."

Sharon did not take well to the idea that her husband could play a little game that put her down so completely. She began a little detective work and soon discovered that in the city from which the couple had come, her husband just happened to have another wife. When she confronted him with the existence of the second wife, he denied it.

Searching for further proof of her husband's bigamy, she was able to make contact with the woman. Then she discovered that the woman knew Pete was married to someone else, but it wasn't Sharon. There was a third wife! Pete was married to three women in three states, and for kicks, he had at least two girlfriends on the side.

The long and bitter procedure of divorce revealed more and more lies. By the time she was free of the marriage, Sharon was so full of bitterness and distrust that she found it impossible to have any close relationships, even with other women. When she finally established what seemed to be a potentially meaningful relationship with a female coworker, she received a new jolt. The woman was a lesbian who nearly raped her one evening.

Sharon became entirely closed to others. Her bitterness took a strange twist, however. She delighted in beginning friendships with other women, only to abandon them as soon as she had won their confidence. In time she turned to men. She was an attractive person who received attention from men rather easily. She deliberately plotted to win their interest and get them into her bed. But once would always be enough. After that she would have nothing to do with them. Next she turned entirely to reading pornographic material and satisfying herself with various forms of masturbation.

Sharon is an extreme example but by no means an isolated case of what bitterness can do to someone's ability to build meaningful relationships. People who feel betrayed and abused will quite naturally draw within themselves for safety. In that state it will not be possible to do the things necessary in wholesome relationships. They cannot take the risk of revealing the inner self to others. They cannot become vulnerable. They cannot trust.

People who cannot trust, however, may still make certain attempts to find sexual pleasure. In Sharon's case sexual pleasure was sought in isolation from others, sexual fantasies, and masturbation. Others who have chosen to become invulnerable have often descended into more self-destructive patterns. In the most extreme cases such people seek sexual pleasure in ways that destroy other people.

It Seemed Easier Before

Several years ago a divorced man came to me for counseling. He had experienced several broken romances since his divorce. It seemed that one way or another something would always go wrong for him in his relationships with women. Inevitably, the problem would have something to do with sex.

"It always seemed easier before," he said.

"What do you mean 'before'?" I asked.

"Before I got married. Back when I was a kid."

I think he was right. As hard as it may have been back when we were kids, there are many ways in which it is a lot harder to understand our sexuality when suddenly we are single again.

One reason is that we have lost our innocence. As kids, we were completely naive. Even if we had had a lot of physical sexual experience before marriage, we were still naive about the depth and variety of meaning of our sexuality. Back in those days we still thought of the world of sexual things in terms of fantasy. We still believed that somewhere "over the rainbow" we would meet that perfect someone, and somehow, automatically, all things sexual would come together for us. In those innocent days of old we knew nothing at all about the hard work required to maintain the pleasure and satisfaction of an ongoing sexual relationship. We knew almost nothing of the need to develop what I have called the spiritual pleasures of sexuality. We really did believe in magic. The love songs and love stories had us convinced that sex was simple. Oh, sure, there would be problems, but our "love" would carry us through.

Divorced people know better. They have been there. They have had those dreams like everyone else, and they have learned the hard way that the real world never measures up to the dreams. They know that mere physical sexual privilege does not have the power to create bliss automatically. Thus, divorced persons are skeptical and cautious about sexuality. Here is a second reason why it is often harder to understand sexuality when one is single again. Maybe all that promised sexual bliss is really out there somewhere. But for the person who is single again, one thing is for sure—it's not automatic.

Losing youthful innocence is not the same thing as growing in wisdom and maturity. Just because we have learned that physical sexual activity alone is not enough to create that elusive bliss does not mean that we have learned much about what does create it. One of the saddest realities that I have seen in counseling with the divorced is the way in which people can repeat their mistakes in this regard.

John used to come to our seminars frequently, but he never learned anything. The first time I met him he had been recently divorced. The next time I met him he had been recently divorced again. The third time he came to the seminar he was close to divorce number three. Each time he would take the elective "Single Sexuality." John never seemed to learn that a meaningful relationship would require more than physical sex.

Again and again John would find a new woman friend. In short order they would find their way into bed. Then it would not be long before John would be alone again. As John would pour out his confusion to me and others, he would point out that his problem was not on the physical level, but on the spiritual level. Physical matters seemed pretty natural for John and his lady friends. But why didn't it ever work?

Once John and I sat at dinner and talked about his struggle.

He asked his usual question, "Why don't things ever work out for me?" "One of the reasons," I responded, "is that you are trying to make a physical sexual involvement carry the weight of a personal relationship. John, that will never work."

"But that's not what I intend to do," he replied. "I've heard what you say about the importance of getting to know someone well and building a relationship of trust and sharing. I believe all of that stuff is really important."

"Then why is it that you seem to land in bed so quickly with every woman you meet?" I asked.

"I don't know," he said. "It just seems so easy. I mean once we get close to each other . . . it just sort of . . . happens."

I felt sorry for John. He was lonely. He was longing for a truly meaningful relationship with a woman, but he was almost entirely lacking in the skills necessary to build a true relationship. And he seemed to have no ability whatsoever to control his sexual impulses. Then he revealed what seemed to be the primary source of his trouble.

"What does it hurt, after all?" he asked. "If a man and a woman want to share an evening together and comfort each other in sexual ways . . . well, what's really wrong with that? Who are they hurting? I mean, so long as they know that they're safe."

There it was: John had no clear moral standard. He was not sure what he believed or how he could go about deciding what he ought to believe. In the end, if no one was getting hurt, what was wrong with his behavior? And why should he work hard to change?

John is by no means alone. Multitudes of single-again people (many of them Christians) are attempting to struggle with their sexuality without any clear moral structure in their minds. They are disillusioned about sexuality and relationships in general, yet they are sexually mature adults whose hearts and bodies ache for the completion that their sexuality calls for. They often lack the skills to build solid personal relationships without becoming entangled in physical sexual involvements. And most important, they are not sure what they believe about sexual morality anyway.

My friend was right. It seemed easier before. But the persons who are single again cannot go back in time. The real questions of who and what we are as sexual beings must be asked. When answers are given, they must speak to the problems faced by my friends in this chapter. What shall we say to Bill who did not recognize the extent of his weakness and vulnerability and thereby fell into a sexual involvement that violated his highest standards?

What is our counsel (perhaps I should say apology) to Debbie who faithfully walked with God and yet found herself suspected, shunned, and discarded by her church because her struggle created uneasiness for them?

What do we have to say to Sharon whose cruel mistreatment caused her to withdraw into isolation and sexual perversion?

And how do we give direction to John who seems to be completely victimized by the sexual brainwashing of our society and the urgency of his passions?

I believe that the answers to all these questions and many others may be found by taking a new look at what God has said to us in His Word. In the holy Scriptures we will find three things I believe are desperately needed by those who seek to find their way in the confusion of today's sexual scene. First, we will find God's affirmation of the sacredness and goodness of human sexuality as He has created it. Second, we will learn the value of the moral standard of God's law both in fulfilling and in protecting us in our sexual pursuits. Third, we will discover the compassion and mercy of God as He reaches out to those who have stumbled and fallen along the way.

5

Relearning
the Rule
of God

A few years ago I had the opportunity to talk with a young
woman who had many questions about sexual morality. What
did the Bible really say about sexual conduct? How could you
know if you loved someone enough to marry? Was it sinful to go to bed
with the person you were going to marry on the next day?

We spent over two hours discussing the answers to these questions.
She was a Christian who seemed to take the Bible seriously. She wanted
real answers, she said. She wanted a moral life. Finally, after I had given
her my very best effort at reasoning for a Christian morality that reserved
intercourse for marriage alone, she summed up her thinking.

"Well, I'm certainly convinced. I'm not having intercourse with anybody until I get married," she said.

I felt genuinely pleased. When we began to talk she had many questions about what she really believed. In two short hours, I had done a
masterful job. Or so I thought. Then she popped my bubble.

"Unless, of course, I really do love him."

This young lady's statement perfectly illustrates the new standard of
morality in our society. Countless single people (one assumes the majority) are now basing the decision about whether or not to have intercourse
on the presence or absence of genuine feelings of love. Beyond that simple
(and exceedingly dangerous) guideline they have no moral standards.
Moral standards may make sense while one is calm, cool, and collected,
but let a rush of "feelings of love" come along and standards can fly out
the window in a moment.

Not only the young are living by this new standard. Older and more mature people, whom one might expect to have more mature methods of making moral decisions, are also discovering that they are ruled by their feelings alone, not by any objective moral framework.

Ed was a fine middle-aged Christian. He had been divorced for about five years and had the custody of his two children. He was a hardworking, churchgoing man of generally high principles. He devoted much of his spare time to outreach and mercy ministries in his church. He was a regular middle-aged Boy Scout.

Ed had been coming to a small group meeting for single men that I conducted in which we regularly discussed sexual questions. He had heard me speak many times on the subject of sexual morality and was fully in agreement that the standard for moral conduct had to be the Word of God. No question about it for Ed. Intercourse outside marriage was wrong. Until Ed met Janet.

"Tom, I've changed my mind about sex before marriage," Ed told me.

"Why?" I asked.

"Well, Tom, if you could just meet her, you would see how right she is for me. I've just never met anyone who seems to understand me so well. It's really good to feel this kind of love."

"I'm sure it is," I said. "How long have you known Janet?"

"Three months," he replied.

I was amazed. I've been around long enough that I shouldn't have been surprised, but I was. I knew Ed to be a solid, down-to-earth fellow. He made decisions carefully and rationally. He always logically carried his principles through to their necessary implications. And there he sat, looking squarely into my eyes, telling me that in three months he had experienced a feeling that had reshaped his moral world.

"Ed," I asked, "have you now decided that God's word to you applies only up to the point that your feelings become highly aroused?"

He smiled. "I guess that's how it sounds to you," he said.

"Well, how does it sound to you?" I inquired. "What you seem to be telling me is that now that you have met this wonderful woman. . . ."

"She is a wonderful woman," he interrupted.

"I'm not saying that she isn't, Ed," I responded. "I don't know her, and I can't comment about what kind of woman she is. I will assume for the moment that she really is all that you think she is. But my question for you remains the same. How does this wonderful woman who appears in your life suddenly change the moral law of God?"

He thought for a moment and said, "Well, of course the law isn't really changed. But it's just that I'm not so sure I really want to wait until we get married." He grinned shyly, as if he had just heard himself say something a little embarrassing.

"Listen to yourself, Ed," I said. "What you are saying is that now that your sexual passions have been aroused, you question the value of the moral law of God. What you are telling me is that you are unwilling to be governed by the rule of God."

"Somehow," he replied, "I just think God understands what I'm feeling."

"What kind of a response is that?" I asked. "Of course God understands your feelings. But can you possibly believe that He approves the breaking of His moral law just because He understands the feelings of a man who is tempted to break that law?"

"I don't know," he said. "I'm just not sure what I believe."

My friend Ed is representative of a vast multitude of people, both young and old, who have lost their moral bearings in the sexual jungle of modern society. Exactly what is right and wrong? And how does one decide? After all, how can something that feels so right be so wrong?

A Question of Rule

The fundamental question I asked Ed is, What rules your conduct? That is the moral question we all must ask. By what rule or standard are we guided? How do we decide questions of a moral nature?

In his book *Sex for Christians*, Dr. Lewis Smedes discusses four broad approaches to making moral decisions. They are (1) the Morality of Caution, (2) the Morality of Concern, (3) the Morality of Personal Relationships, and (4) the Morality of Law.[1]

Whether we have spent much time seriously thinking about it or not, we all make moral choices based on one or more of these approaches. It will be helpful to examine ourselves and our moral decisions in the light of these options.

In using the *Morality of Caution* individuals ask only one simple question: Will I get hurt? The only concern is personal well-being and safety. This is the basis of the much-publicized safe-sex campaigns of our day. It would be foolish to have sexual relations with a disease-carrying person. So, be safe. Know your partner. Use condoms.

The Morality of Caution is smart; it is, however, the lowest form of morality. It is basically self-centered and self-serving. It takes care of number one, but does not reach further than that. It is entirely inadequate as a basis for a truly moral life.

The *Morality of Concern* goes a step higher. On this level persons consider the consequences their actions may have on the lives of others. Here the question becomes, If we have sexual relations, what will it do to my partner? In the "old" days a man would perhaps refrain from intercourse because he did not want to get a woman pregnant. The widespread availability of modern contraceptives has nearly eliminated this problem.

Still, sensitive people may concern themselves with what their sexual actions may do to others. What emotional consequences may result from having sexual intercourse? How will my partner feel after we do this? Will there be embarrassment? regret? a bad conscience? Persons guided by the Morality of Concern will not wish to do anything that has the potential to trouble or weaken a partner's life.

In addition, since there are usually no absolute guarantees that protect from pregnancy, the question must be asked, What if there a child is conceived? Would it be good for this child to be born to these parents at this time? What kind of parents would we make? What kind of life would this child have? In the event of the birth of an unexpected child to unmarried parents there are also the questions of the effects on other family members, friends, and the community.

Persons who care deeply about the effects of their actions on others may refrain from sexual intercourse for that reason. The Morality of Concern, therefore, protects others from certain forms of injury. But it does not give sufficient guidance to persons seeking a true moral principle.

The *Morality of Personal Relationships* raises us to an even higher level. Here, the question asked is, What effect would sexual intercourse have upon our relationship? This approach recognizes that the truest measure of who and what we are is our relationships. I can come to know and truly understand myself only by inquiring into the nature of the relationships in which I am involved. Therefore, I want my actions to enhance and strengthen my personal relationships. Any action that would likely weaken or damage personal relationships would, on this basis, be immoral. Such actions would injure others and myself.

It is certainly commendable to concern ourselves with the quality of our personal relationships and to hold ourselves responsible within our relationships. But the basic problem with this approach as a basis for moral decision making is that it is impossible to apply. There is simply no way that we can know in advance how a particular action will later affect the quality of a relationship. We can only guess about what will happen, take the action, and then wait and see.

As a pastoral counselor, I can attest to the fact that many people are surprised by the results of their sexual decisions.

Several years ago Dan came to see me about his relationship with Darlene. She had really changed recently, and he wasn't sure just what had gone wrong.

"Dan, have you and Darlene been sleeping together?" I asked.

"Yes," he said.

"Is there any connection between that and the change in Darlene's attitude as far as you can tell?"

"Yes, I think so," he answered. "I think it was right away after we began to have intercourse that she began to get . . . I don't know . . . moody."

"Explain what you mean by moody." I said.

"Well, it's hard to explain," he continued. "She just seemed real sad sometimes. No, most of the time. It was like I couldn't do anything to please her. I mean, she wanted me around more than before. She didn't want to break up or anything. In fact, she began to talk a lot about getting married."

"How do you feel about getting married?" I asked.

"I don't think we're ready for that," he said. "I need a better job, and she's still pretty young. And . . . well, there's just a lot of questions about our relationship, especially since she's started acting so funny."

Dan and Darlene did not know in advance what it would be like after they had intercourse. Afterward it was too late to go back where they had been before. She had new insecurities about where their relationship was headed and wanted the security of a promise of marriage. Dan did not understand her insecurities very well and reacted to what he interpreted as pressure from Darlene. For a while they continued to sleep together. Eventually, Darlene asked that they stop. Dan hung around for a few weeks but, finally, decided to look elsewhere.

There were no diseases for Dan or Darlene. There was no unwanted pregnancy (one can only thank God). And there was no public or family embarrassment. But the emotional and spiritual scars were very real. They lost their ability to trust each other and soon were unable to communicate. Their physical passion abated, and they had nothing left but pain and disappointment.

These first three approaches to establishing a sexual moral principle do not seem to get us very far. They seem to ask only one basic question: What does it hurt? If we could know that our sexual adventures would not hurt us, that they would not harm someone else, or that they would not weaken our personal relationships, it seems that sexual intercourse outside marriage would be permissible. But these are precisely the things that we cannot know in advance, so we have been given no help.

There is one additional problem with these approaches to sexual morality. They treat sexual intercourse as if it has no moral significance. They do not ask questions about the nature of the act of intercourse.

Dr. Smedes comments on this basic error:

> Each of the three moralities for sexual intercourse focuses on factors outside of the act itself. None of them assumes that sexual intercourse has a built-in factor that in itself would disqualify unmarried people for it. But Christian morality has traditionally believed that there is such a factor. For it has maintained that, even if nobody gets hurt and even if a personal relationship could be enriched by it, it is wrong for all but married people.[2]

These usual approaches to sexual morality mistakenly assume that sexual intercourse in itself has no meaning. It may have moral significance if it results in someone's being harmed, but in itself it is believed to be morally neutral.

We must move on, then, to consider the *Morality of Law*. In this approach the assumption is made that the only way to know what is morally correct is to listen to the law of God. Of course, many in our society have been unwilling to make that assumption. There are those, in the first place, who do not believe in God. There are others who believe in Him, but do not believe that He has clearly spoken. There are still others who seem to believe that God has spoken in the past but somehow has changed His opinion as frequently as we have in recent days.

It is my belief that God exists and that He has spoken plainly in the holy Scriptures. More than that, I believe that the Scriptures are infallible and, therefore, provide for all mankind an entirely reliable foundation of moral truth. I am assuming that most of my readers will agree with me at this point or, at least, will listen with an open mind now that they understand my particular frame of reference.

Once we have granted that God is really there, and that He really has spoken truth to man, we are ready for the Morality of Law. In listening to the Morality of Law for our guidance, we accept the idea that our sexuality is a part of the way the good God of heaven created us. We make the additional assumption that God alone knows the true nature and purpose of our sexuality.

If intrinsic meaning and value are in the act of sexual intercourse, therefore, they are there because God placed them there. In learning from God, then, we will learn the truth about what we are as sexual beings as well as the purposes for which He created us.

To choose to make our moral decisions on the basis of the law of God, then, becomes *an act of faith*. Faith includes both belief and commitment. Christian faith is first of all the belief that the God of the Bible exists and that we humans truly are His creatures. It also means that we accept God's rule over our lives as legitimate and binding. Finally, it means that we commit ourselves to living in accordance with His will. Therefore, we choose lives of obedience because such lives both honor God and bring fulfillment and satisfaction to us.

The Bible and Sexuality

A few months ago I was talking with a professional sex therapist about the basis for making decisions regarding sexual morality. When I mentioned that I tried to get my guidance from the Bible, he was amused. "Sure," he said, "that's like the mice taking safety lessons from the cat, isn't it?"

This man's attitude toward the Bible is typical of that of many people. Their perception of biblical teachings is usually negative. They probably haven't actually read the Bible. But their minds are made up. In their opinion, the Bible's teachings about sexuality are negative and narrow.

These people would be very surprised to learn how positively the Bible treats human sexuality. The Scriptures present sexuality as a natural part of the good creation of God, given to us for the furtherance and nurture of our lives, and celebrated and sanctified as something especially significant to God Himself.

God's Affirmation of Sexuality

We must not get the idea that somehow when God accidentally created sexuality, He embarrassed Himself, turned red, and hid His face. The account of the creation of the first man and woman in the book of Genesis makes it clear that God created the woman intentionally to be mate to the man. Having created them "in the image of God" (Gen. 1:27), God then looked upon all His creation, "and it was very good" (Gen. 1:31).

If we had no more information than those two references, we would see that sexuality is given a natural and proper place in the order of the good things God made. But there is much more.

Chapter 2 of Genesis states in more detail that it was God's will for the man and the woman to be "joined" and "become one flesh" (v. 24). Then we learn that the man and his wife "were both naked," and they "were not ashamed" (v. 25). The writer seems to emphasize there was nothing wrong with that original nakedness. It was not shameful to them, and it was not shameful before God. They were created naked, their nakedness was created for each other, and it was very good.

We should also be encouraged to observe that before human sin entered the picture, God commanded the man and the woman to have intercourse. God blessed them and said to them, "Be fruitful and multiply" (Gen. 1:28).

There is not the slightest suggestion in this account of the creation of sexuality that God has a negative attitude toward sexual matters. God is the Author of sexuality. He invented it. He blessed it. And He loves it. We must assume that when Adam and Eve engaged in sexual intercourse, God was delighted with what He had made and considered it very good.

Other biblical references to sexuality indicate that within the context of marriage, great delight should be taken in this special form of union God has given to man and woman. Proverbs 5:18–19 enjoins the young husband,

> Rejoice with the wife of your youth.
> As a loving deer and a graceful doe,
> Let her breasts satisfy you at all times;
> And always be enraptured with her love.

The Song of Solomon is entirely devoted to the celebration of the sexual love of King Solomon and his bride. The language of the book is so explicitly sexual, even passionate, that generations of Christians have avoided its obvious meaning and taught that it was intended only to symbolize the love of God for His people.

Even if we were to accept the interpretation that the love portrait of the Song was meant by God to be a symbol only, the teaching is still an implicit approval of sexual love. Would God use a symbol that was impure? Of course not. The truth is precisely opposite to such thinking. God has chosen the celebration of sexual love for inclusion in His Word because He loves and honors it as a high and beautiful part of His creation.

Some explicit New Testament passages speak in positive ways about the value of sexual love between married persons. The writer to the Hebrews says, "Marriage is honorable among all, and the bed undefiled; but fornicators and adulterers God will judge" (Heb. 13:4). Marriage and the marriage bed are honorable! And that is the very reason why God speaks so severely about persons who violate the honor and the purity of marriage. God honors married sexual love because He designed it for His own special purpose. The terrible judgment of God mentioned here is no condemnation of sexuality—it is condemnation of the *violation* of sexuality.

God even speaks encouragingly to husbands and wives who, for whatever reasons, might deprive each other of the sexual privilege:

> Let the husband render to his wife the affection due her, and likewise also the wife to her husband. The wife does not have authority over her own body, but the husband does. And likewise the husband does not have authority over his own body, but the wife does. Do not deprive one another except with consent for a time, that you may give yourselves to fasting and prayer; and come together again so that Satan does not tempt you because of your lack of self-control (1 Cor. 7:3-5).

It would be impossible to read these passages and conclude that God disapproves our sexuality. The Bible uniformly affirms the basic goodness of our maleness and femaleness, and of our physical sexual union. Sexual intercourse itself is affirmed. It is the gift of God and is always viewed in an honorable way by the biblical writers.

But why does God say that sexual intercourse belongs exclusively within the framework of marriage? Is there some special ingredient in the very nature of sexual intercourse that makes it improper outside the marriage bond? What is that ingredient? What is it about sexual intercourse that causes God to require a man and a woman to marry before they may express their love in this way? Or what is it about marriage that somehow adds the ingredient of honor to the sexual union?

One Flesh

God commands that sexual union should be reserved only for the married because of what the Bible calls the one-flesh union. God created sexuality for the purpose of bringing a man and a woman together in a whole-life union of body and soul. This union makes the two of them one flesh.

When God created the woman and took her to Adam, Adam called her "flesh of my flesh" (Gen. 2:23). We are then told, "Therefore a man shall leave his father and mother and be joined to his wife, and they shall become one flesh" (Gen. 2:24).

The concept of one flesh does not express to the modern reader of English nearly what it expressed in the Hebrew language in which Genesis is written. The Hebrew word *flesh* meant "man" or "human life." A good example of this usage is found in the words of the prophet Isaiah, who said that "all flesh is grass"(40:6). The meaning is that all men's lives are short. *Flesh* in this sense means "mankind."

When we are told, therefore, that a man and a woman may unite and become one flesh, the meaning is that the two lives become one. The coming together of their two bodies in sexual union points to the coming together of their two souls, their two spirits, their two lives! That was God's intention when He created them male and female. The purpose of sexual intercourse, then, is the union of lives.

The one-flesh concept becomes the basis upon which Christian morality is built. In writing to the young Corinthian church, the apostle Paul says,

> Do you not know that your bodies are members of Christ? Shall I then take the members of Christ and make them members of a harlot? Certainly not! Or do you not know that he who is joined to a harlot is one body with her? For "The two," He says, "shall become one flesh." But he who is joined to the Lord is one spirit with Him (1 Cor. 6:15-17).

The Corinthians to whom Paul was writing lived in a culture that believed bodily actions were relatively unimportant. The body was only matter; it would perish. But the soul was preeminent. One could rationalize that what a person did with the body was of little concern so long as the soul was not involved. Some new Christians who engaged in sex with prostitutes believed that no harm was done.

Paul was outraged! Because he understood the way God created man and woman, Paul understood the meaning of sexual union to be the bringing together of two lives in the pledge of permanent love. He saw the illogic (indeed, the sin) of what the Corinthians were trying to do. They were engaging their bodies in sexual unions with women *without the intention of uniting their lives with them!*

The Corinthians were behaving as if sexual intercourse had no essential meaning in itself and could be used in any way that proved enjoyable. This is precisely the attitude of many people in our modern society. The assumption is that sexual intercourse means only what two consenting adults determine it will mean.

To Paul, however, to enter into a physical, sexual union without the intention of entering into a life-union was to violate God's creation. Nothing short of the marriage commitment can legitimize sexual union. Marriage alone can bring honor to sexual intercourse because God has created sexuality to be a life-bond involving both body and soul. Marriage, and only marriage, brings the life-uniting intention alongside the life-uniting act.

Do I Accept God?

The question of morality, then, is ultimately a question of faith. Do I believe in God? Do I accept God? Do I accept the law of God as my own standard and guide in matters of sexuality? Do I believe that God is the Creator of my sexual nature, and that He knows better than I do what is right and good for me? Do I believe that I am obligated to present my life (soul and body) to God in faith and obedience?

Once again, we will benefit from the instruction of the apostle Paul:

> For this is the will of God, your sanctification: that you should abstain from sexual immorality; that each of you should know how to possess his own vessel in sanctification and honor, not in passion of lust, like the Gentiles who do not know God; that no one should take advantage of and defraud his brother in this matter, because the Lord is the avenger of all such, as we also forewarned you and testified. For God did not call us to uncleanness, but in holiness. Therefore he who rejects this does not reject man, but God, who has also given us His Holy Spirit (1 Thess. 4:3–8).

In this passage Paul teaches that the foundation of sexual morality for Christians is the "will of God." God wants us to accept Him and to honor His will for our lives, which means that we must accept His teachings about sexuality. We must not permit ourselves to be ruled by our "lusts" in the way that others are. Instead, we are to control our bodies in a holy and honorable way. We are not to do anything that would wrong our brother (or sister). To reject this moral instruction is to reject God Himself.

This last instruction gives us the definitive answer to the question, What does it hurt? It hurts God. Even if we could somehow prove that no one else would be hurt by sexual union outside marriage (and we can never prove that), God would be hurt. He would be hurt because our disobedience rejects Him personally.

The greatest and highest reason for moral behavior is to honor and please God. Believers do not accept the rule of God out of some slavish discipline to obey rules for rules' sake. Rather, we obey the rule of God because we love Him and want to please Him. The words of the apostle John ring true in the depths of every Christian heart: "For this is the love of God, that we keep His commandments. And His commandments are not burdensome" (1 John 5:3).

God's commands are no burden for sincere Christians. Quite the contrary, to us the laws of God are a delight because in keeping them we show our love to God. That was Paul's meaning when he wrote to the Corinthians about their sexual immorality. How could they who were "members of Christ" and "one spirit with Him" (1 Cor. 6:15, 17) be united sexually with prostitutes? To do so would be to personally injure their Lord.

For Christians, then, making moral choices is a matter of loving and pleasing God. Because we love God and desire to please Him, we accept the rule of God's Word in our daily lives. Accepting God's Word as the basis for moral decisions lifts us out of the modern swampland of "feelings" and sets us on a solid foundation of truth. Right and wrong are determined by the will of God, not by our rapidly changing emotions or cultural mood swings.

Therefore, on the basis of God's truth we may know without question when our feelings are leading us toward a wrong decision. Certain things are always wrong and always displease the Lord, no matter how tempting they may seem at the moment. We usually find this easier to accept when we are tempted by the stronger negative emotions.

For example, I may be enraged by the driver who cuts in front of me in traffic, but I know it would be wrong to follow my rage and shoot him dead. I also know that even though I desperately want a turkey for Thanksgiving dinner, it would be wrong for me to steal one because I can't afford to buy one. Murder and stealing are wrong, and I must not permit my momentary emotions to cause me to do such things.

However, when we are tempted by more positive emotions, such as feelings of love and sexual desire, it may be more difficult to see the need for resisting and controlling our actions. At this point love for God and confidence in the law of God give us clear and definite guidance. *Even good feelings may lead us to actions that would displease our loving God.* The popular old verse, "It can't be wrong when it feels so right," may feel right—but it's wrong!

The Safety of Obedience

Furthermore, to accept God's rule makes us safe. First of all, it sets us right before God. To come to God with a heart of faith and obedience pleases Him and results in His blessing on our lives. But to disobey God brings us under His judgment and makes us liable for punishment.

Second, when we accept God's rule for our conduct, we will not risk injuring ourselves or others. One rarely hears of persons who have walked faithfully with God wishing that they had been less moral. But there are many stories of persons who have behaved immorally and would give anything to go back in time and undo some immoral conduct.

The safety that the moral law of God provides may be better understood if we compare it to natural law. When we speak of the "laws" of nature, we are describing only the "way things are." For example, to speak of the law of gravity is only to say that things happen in a certain way. Whatever has weight will fall toward the center of the earth. That's the way it is, and we can benefit from knowing that it is so.

Let us say that I choose to reject the law of gravity and step off the top of the Empire State Building to get a better view. One might say that I had chosen to break the law. But it would be more likely that the law would continue to function just fine and that I would be the broken one. The law will not change just because one day I decide to violate it. It is still the law, and it will have its way with me even if I go against it.

It is the same with God's moral law. It simply describes the way things are in God's moral universe. If I reject the law and live as if it were not true, I will be the one broken. I will lose the blessing of God, I will likely injure other people, and I will most certainly bring harm upon myself.

I am reminded of a cartoon I saw some months ago. A youngster is standing beside his grandfather who is reclining in an easy chair with his newspaper. The boy asks, "Grandpa, in your day, what did you wear for safe sex?"

His grandfather replies, "A wedding ring."

Only a casual look at today's society will reveal the wisdom in Grandpa's remark. Because we have forsaken the belief that marriage is a necessary part of "safe sex," we have turned away from commitment. Unwittingly, we have forsaken safety as well. The inability of lovers to keep their promises to each other has caused more and more "experts" to advise people that it is good to have sexual relationships without making promises. The resultant sexual "freedom" of our day has created a climate in which the only sexual goal is physical pleasure. But physical sex alone soon becomes boring and drives us to new partners and new twists. The rapid increase in pornography, sex clubs, sex experimentation, and even sex crimes (not to mention the incredible epidemic of sexual disease) is directly related to our abandonment of the moral law of God. Most significant, the loss of spiritual standards has resulted in the loss of satisfaction and contentment. Grandpa was right. Only marriage provides safe sex.

1. Smedes, *Sex for Christians,* p. 115.
2. Ibid., p. 125.

6

Is There Life Without Sex?

A young woman named Carol sat across from me looking like she had just seen her first Martian. She had heard me speak at a seminar on sexuality and had been amazed to hear a modern man speak in favor of "old-fashioned" morality as I had. She had come to see me in person to ask some very specific questions about what I believed. My answers had followed the line of reasoning presented in the last chapter.

"I just don't believe what I'm hearing," she said. "You're telling me that now that I'm alone I'm condemned to a life without sex."

"I'm telling you what God's Word teaches," I replied. "That is, sexual intercourse is the symbol of married love, and only those who make the commitment of marriage have the right to it."

"So my ex-husband gets to sleep around all he wants because he could care less about God, and I have to sit at home and twiddle my thumbs because of what the Bible says?"

"I am not approving what your ex-husband is doing," I said. "Certainly he is violating God's Word by his behavior, and I believe that there will be consequences he will have to face. But I am saying that unless you marry again, you should stay out of bed with a man."

"Because I love God, right?" she said angrily.

"Carol," I asked, "do you love God?"

She began to weep in a mixture of frustration and hurt. After a time she looked at me and said, "Right now, I don't know. I used to love Him. I just never expected to be where I am right now."

"Tell me where you are," I said.

"I'm lonely, and I hurt," she said through more tears, "and I just need somebody who cares about me. I just need to be held once in a while. I always enjoyed all that physical stuff, and I miss it. What's wrong with that?"

I had been exactly where she was, and my heart cried out for her and with her as she spoke. I replied, "Carol, nothing is wrong with the needs you feel. They are normal and natural. You are feeling what anyone in your situation would feel. And God Himself understands those feelings."

"I'm sure He does," she said bitterly. "So just what does He expect me to do with all this hurt in here? Tom, I'm a grown woman with a grown woman's needs, and I'm not capable of being a nun."

"I think there are answers to your needs," I said, "but breaking God's moral law is not one of them."

At that her patience broke and she stood up to leave.

"I guess I just don't understand you or God," she said. Then she walked out.

I wish I could tell you there was a happy sequel to that meeting, but there was not. Carol never came back to see me. A few months later a friend of hers told me that she was living with a male friend. The needs she felt had won out over her interest in knowing and loving God.

Carol is one among many single-again persons facing the enormous pressures of what to do about their frustrated sexual needs. Even people with the very highest Christian standards often have great struggles in making the sexual adjustment to single life after having been married.

The Need for Intimacy

The most obvious part of that adjustment process is found in the normal need for intimacy. That need does not go away when a divorce occurs. In fact, it intensifies because of the sense of rejection and failure these people experience. And regardless of how sexually active they may have been, married persons have been accustomed to the freedom of sexual intimacy whenever the time was right. In other words, when the moment was mutually agreeable, the hearts tender and warm, and the spirits in tune, the bodies naturally followed along.

Persons who are single again do not instantly lose their sexual history. They are accustomed to expressing intimate feelings in physical ways. Add to that the intense loneliness and lack of self-esteem that they usually experience and the result is often a kind of sexual dynamite just waiting for a match.

The match may come along in the form of a genuinely caring person whose compassion reaches out to help a hurting friend. That was the case for my friend Bill, mentioned in chapter 4. When he and Judy began to talk to each other after his divorce, Bill was not thinking of another relationship. Neither of them expected to fall in love. But it happened, and when it did, it immediately found full sexual expression.

Bill and Judy were both professing Christian people with strong moral beliefs. Neither of them had ever behaved immorally before. Suddenly, they were sleeping together and hardly knowing how they had crossed the line into forbidden things.

The Absence of Moral Maturity

Another factor in the lives of single-again persons is the absence of true moral maturity. That is, many of these people married young, say at eighteen to twenty, and actually have very little experience dealing with the discipline of sexual morality as mature persons. Soon after high school they took the plunge into marriage—everybody was doing it—and they were faithful to their mates. These people likely have thought little about how moral principles apply to sexually mature people.

Young people, for example, often behave morally without examining their reasons thoroughly. They may stay out of bed only out of fear of disease or pregnancy. If their moral thinking progressed no further than that before they were married, and they were married at twenty and divorced at thirty-three, they will probably find that their old reasons for morality are not much help at this new stage in their lives.

It is not surprising, then, that these lonely people, hungry for someone to care for them, relatively inexperienced in mature sexual discipline, and flooded with the enticements and encouragement of our sexually liberated age, will often flounder when faced with sexual decisions as mature single people.

Disillusionment

Another part of the sexual struggle for single-again persons is disillusionment. Many people have faithfully embraced traditional Christian morality in a naive way. One does not have intercourse until marriage because God says so. Although this belief may have been easily accepted in youth, it may not be helpful to more mature persons because of the bitterness of their experience.

Eric was a fine Christian man who had married young, faithfully loved his wife for twenty years, and recently been divorced.

"Quite frankly, I would like for God to give me an explanation," he said to me as we sipped our coffee together.

"Go on," I said.

"Well, what's this all about anyway?" he asked. "I have loved and served God as faithfully as I've known how ever since I was a kid. I read Christian books on how to be a good husband before we got married. I worked hard at doing what was right. I was always faithful to her, Tom. I had opportunities when I was traveling, but I never fell off the fidelity wagon. I knew it was wrong. Now, this is my reward, I guess."

"Eric, I know how you feel," I told him. "All I can say to you is that God knows you were faithful. And I'm sure He is pleased with the way you have lived."

"Well, I just don't know if that's good enough anymore," he said. "I'm not so sure it works."

What Eric said has been said by many and thought by millions. If I do things God's way, isn't it supposed to mean that a few rewards come my way? What kind of God is He anyway? Am I supposed to serve Him for nothing?

I have full understanding and deep feeling for these people. In many ways their story is my story. I have felt their pain, asked their questions, and wrestled for moral strength just as they have. My primary reason for writing this book is to offer some help to individuals struggling with questions such as these.

I hope that my attempts to help will not seem simplistic or uncompassionate. What I have to say about readjustment to single life grows entirely out of my personal experience. I was a single man for fourteen years before I remarried. During those years I sometimes failed to follow God's moral principles. I have only sorrow in admitting that, but I mention it both to indicate that I understand weakness and to encourage others who may have failed. By God's great grace and with the aid of many Christian friends (especially the devoted Christian woman who was to become my wife), I grew to be a contented single man long before I remarried. I learned things about the meaning of my sexuality that I had never learned before. I learned how to appreciate and enjoy my sexuality more fully than I ever had, even though I did not have the privilege of full sexual expression.

A man once asked me, "Can there really be life without sex?" What he meant was, Is it possible to have a happy life without the privilege of intercourse? I have learned that the answer is a resounding "Yes." The loss of the sexual privilege is not the loss of life. It may bring pain, but it does not bring death. Indeed, for those who will take the opportunity, it can open doors for growth into sexual maturity and enjoyment that they might never have reached any other way.

A New Look at Singleness

Singles groups have become fond of affirming that "one is a whole number." It certainly is. And it is just as true that one person, though unmarried and "uninvolved," may be whole and happy. But it is painful for divorced people (whether they chose the divorce of not) to have singleness thrust upon them. Singleness itself is not the problem, but it may feel like it is. Singleness, for these persons, most likely will not feel like wholeness.

Single-again people may find it difficult to get into the mood to celebrate singleness. Undoubtedly, they chose at one time to be married and live happily ever after. For the majority of us, marriage was always set before us as *the way* to find happiness. Most of us grew up believing that the process was rather automatic. It went something like this—childhood, youth, graduation, marriage = HAPPINESS! Simple.

Single-again people know very well that marriage is no stepping stone into the magic kingdom of perfect happiness, but that does not mean they suddenly redirect their happiness formulas toward singleness. For some, singleness may be only a symbol of marriage failure. To admit to being single may be the ultimate embarrassment. For others, singleness may be a living punishment, a hammer of rejection that beats a daily blow of unworth and guilt into the soul.

It is essential, therefore, that the single-again person take a new look at singleness, for it is true that *wholeness is possible* whether one is married or not. Marriage cannot automatically produce wholeness within the individual, and singleness does not automatically mean unwholeness.

Many of the identity struggles faced by single-again persons come about because we have never been given a healthy and balanced view of singleness. When we were growing up, most of us thought of staying single as the ultimate curse. If you weren't married by the time you were twenty-five, your family and friends made not-so-subtle comments to you indicating something was wrong with you. Marriage was viewed as normal; singleness was abnormal.

Singleness is *not* abnormal, and it is not necessarily a second-class way to live. It is true that marriage has been the route chosen by the vast majority of the population, primarily because of the sexual attraction between man and woman. There are many ways in which we feel that we will be completed in sexual union. But it is a mistake to believe that personal completion can be found only in marriage.

It is also a mistake to believe that the only possible way to be sexually fulfilled is to be married (that is, to have the privilege of full physical sexual expression). Certainly, we have ample proof in our day and age that marriage is no automatic guarantee of sexual fulfillment. Even those who are extremely active sexually are often quite unfulfilled. Sexual fulfillment has to do with far more than whether or not one has the privilege of sexual intercourse.

In fact, a very high degree of sexual fulfillment is possible for single persons who believe and obey God's laws because *sexual fulfillment depends much more upon their knowledge of themselves and the quality of their personal relationships than upon the physical sexual involvement they may have*. Singles who learn to accept God's rule over their singleness and to invest themselves in responsible personal relationships may discover that they are more sexually fulfilled than they were while married. To attain sexual fulfillment, however, people need understanding of the teaching of the Scriptures in regard to singleness and the development of responsible relationships.

God's Word and Singleness

Christians have a preeminent reason for seeing singleness as a good, happy, and fulfilling way to live. Jesus, the Savior, was single throughout His life. In the Scriptures nothing indicates that His singleness was a special burden to Him or that it hindered Him in any way. And He was a sexual being!

Although the Bible nowhere discusses the matter of Christ's sexuality, it affirms that He was fully man (Phil. 2:7–8) and that He faced exactly the same temptations you and I do (Heb. 4:15). We have every reason, therefore, to believe that Jesus, in His earthly life, felt the normal tug of sexual desire and interest. Yet, the Bible says that He faced every temptation without sinning against God (Heb. 4:15).

Approaching the sexuality of Jesus as if it involved only His ability to resist sinful urges would be a mistake. We must assume that He was a man fulfilled in every respect, including His sexual nature! His fulfillment was not merely the virtue of staying out of bed with a woman. It also concerned His ability to relate deeply and lovingly with people He knew—and many of those were women.

Often people will say that it is a small comfort knowing that Jesus successfully lived with sexual needs. Jesus, after all, was also God. I'm not God; I don't have that kind of strength, they assert.

But there are mere men in Scripture who chose to be celibate to accomplish the purposes of God in their lives. Most notable among them was the apostle Paul who argued that the celibate life enabled persons to focus their interests on the work of God's kingdom without the hindrances of married life (1 Cor. 7:32–35).

Paul did not exalt the celibate life above married life. He recognized that not everyone would want to be unmarried or would even possess the strength to remain unmarried. But he and others like him chose to live as single people to accomplish what they believed God had called them to do. It was not considered unusual or heroic to choose the single life. It was a matter of understanding what God wanted to accomplish in one's life.

The same principle is seen in Jesus' teaching when He said that some people "have renounced marriage because of the kingdom of heaven" (Matt. 19:12 NIV). Singleness is not a lesser state of living than marriage. Nor is it a state of extreme deprivation. It is a way of life that may be chosen willingly and lived honorably for the cause of the kingdom of heaven.

The Gift of Singleness

Speaking of his singleness, Paul declares, "I wish that all men were even as I myself" (1 Cor. 7:7), but he continues, "Each one has his own gift from God." Later in chapter 7 Paul indicates that everyone "should remain in the situation which he was in when God called him" (v. 20 NIV).

He means that all people are presently living with certain specific situations and relationships. For example, some are married, and some are single. But persons should be content with their situations before God. Married people should not seek a divorce, and single people should not seek to marry (v. 27).

There is nothing wrong with getting married. Paul recognizes that some people are better suited for married life than for single life. But some people are single, and it is possible for them to serve God responsibly right now. It would be wrong for them to frantically search after a marriage partner as if marriage were the ultimate answer to their needs or as if their singleness somehow prevented them from serving God faithfully.

According to Paul, there are practical ways in which it may actually be to one's advantage to remain single. Single persons do not face the burdens and responsibilities that married life brings with it. The freedom of singleness opens many doors (especially for Christian service) that married persons simply do not have open to them.

Paul's teaching has a wonderfully positive emphasis: "This I say for your own profit, not that I may put a leash on you, but for what is proper, and that you may serve the Lord without distraction" (1 Cor. 7:35). Paul does not perceive the single life to be negative in any way. For him, it is not a life of restriction, but a life of freedom and opportunity. Singleness is a gift from God.

Do You Have the Gift of Singleness?

Christian singles often discuss this matter of the gift of singleness. On occasion I have heard Christian people declare that they do not have the gift of singleness, thereby reasoning that they can't be expected to live by the laws of God regarding sexual behavior.

I had never really thought about the meaning of the so-called gift of singleness until a friend asked me if I possessed it.

"Tom, do you have the gift of singleness?" Dick asked.

I had been single for about twelve years at the time. I had also been seeing Reidun for eight years (two years later we would be married). My friend seemed genuinely concerned about the sexual tension with which he assumed I was living. That was the apparent reason for his question.

I remember being quite taken back by his question. I could not remember ever asking myself the question. I fumbled around for a reply and finally said, "I'm not even sure what that means."

"Well," he said, "I mean can you live the rest of your life as a single man without yielding to sex?"

I thought seriously about what he was asking and gave the only answer that made any sense to me. "I believe that God will give me the strength to do whatever He requires me to do," I said.

"I don't know," he said while shaking his head slowly. "I just don't know."

"Tell me what you're thinking," I asked.

"I'm thinking that you are a man who ought to be married," he answered.

"Dick," I replied, "right now it is simply not possible for us to be married. Perhaps someday, down the road, we may marry. But for now we are single people. And we are single people who know the will of God and are determined to honor Him in our relationship. So far God has given us the strength we need to do just that. I see no reason to doubt that He will continue to strengthen us. I guess that must be the gift of singleness."

"But, Tom," he said, with a look of deep concern, "you are a man who obviously desires female companionship."

"Sure do," I replied.

"And you look pretty healthy to me," he continued.

I took that to mean he supposed I had normal sexual interests and urges.

"Of course I do," I answered.

"Then I don't think you have the gift of singleness," he concluded.

"Which means what?" I inquired.

"It means I think you two should get married," he responded.

As I said, Reidun and I had been seeing each other for eight years by that time. So I was already accustomed to well-meaning people strongly suggesting that we *should* get married. But those people weren't actually living with the specific realities in our two lives that made it very clear to us that marriage was not God's plan for us then. Therefore, they could easily make decisions for us. I just smiled.

But Dick had raised an interesting point. What is the gift of singleness? Did I possess it? After considerable study of both the Bible's teaching and my personal life, I reached some conclusions I will share with you.

First of all, Paul did not actually use the phrase "the gift of singleness" as if there were some special package from heaven that could arrive at the door labeled THE GIFT OF SINGLENESS. If there were, persons could know quite easily that they did, indeed, possess the gift. They could then tell their friends, "I have the gift of singleness."

Most gifts from God are not so easily and immediately recognized by persons possessing them. Of course, some gifts, the kind we might call talents, such as a musical aptitude and a gregarious personality, are easily recognizable. But the realization that we possess other gifts from God may be harder to come by.

Sometimes we possess gifts we do not know we have until some opportunity arises and someone else notices that we are effective at something. Perhaps we never before had that particular opportunity. However, we see what needs to be done, and we do our best. Someone else sees what we did and then tell us we did very well. It appears we are gifted. As a good friend of mine likes to say, "If a job needs to be done, and you can do it—you're gifted!"

Second, it also appears to me that many times what we call gifts could be more properly called graces. Here is what I mean. Do you, for example, have the gift of enduring the disease of cancer for twenty years? Do you have the gift of losing your job? Do you have the gift of facing the death of one of your children?

These possibilities are frightening. No one wants to have to cope with any of these things. They would be very difficult, and we could easily imagine that we would not have the strength to bear up under their weight. Yet, at this moment, I am not facing any of these things. So how can I answer the question about whether or not I have the gifts to face them?

I think it is better to say that if some trouble besets me, through faith I must believe that God will give me the grace to bear it and to turn it into an opportunity to praise and serve Him. This seems to fit the biblical teaching regarding how God's people stand strong in times of hardship and suffering.

I think of the tribulations of Job, who suffered the destruction of his crops, the deaths of his children, and the loss of his physical health. The agony he endured is almost impossible to imagine. And yet, because God was with him and gave him the strength he needed, Job was able to go through all his troubles without sinning against God. (Read at least Job 1:1—2:10.)

Did Job have the gifts of losing crops, children, and health? Obviously, he did. But he probably didn't know that he had them until he actually faced those difficulties. In fact, he probably didn't actually have the gifts until he needed them. That is why I prefer to call Job's special strengths graces. In Job's time of special need, God gave him enabling grace.

Perhaps the outstanding example of this kind of enablement in the New Testament is in Paul's experience. Paul suffered from a great difficulty he called "a thorn in the flesh" (2 Cor. 12:7-10). Bible scholars don't really know what it was, although the majority seem to agree that it was a debilitating eye disease. At any rate, Paul did not like it and prayed for God to remove it from his life. Instead, God gave him the grace to accept it and live contentedly with it.

The lesson is this: many times we will have to face things that are not of our choosing. They will seem too burdensome to bear, and we will recoil from them. We may cry out to God to deliver us from the awful prospect of living with the terrible reality. But God's answer may be to give us the grace to accept the trouble and even find ways to use it for His glory.

These lessons from the lives of Job and Paul can give us insight into the gift of singleness. Singleness may be forced upon people in a way that causes disappointment or even despondency. Many people grew up hoping to get married someday, only to discover later that they would always be single. It was not what they had originally wanted. They may even have prayed that God would send them a marriage partner. But He gave them the grace of singleness instead.

The same thing may apply to persons who have been divorced. They originally planned to be married "happily ever after," but now they are single, and very often, they do not want the single life. They may even pray that God will change things and send their mate back to them or else provide a new one. Instead God may give them the grace of singleness.

I must say this as strongly as possible: Christians have the promise of God that no matter what we have to face, God will always give us the grace to deal with it so that we will not be defeated or forced to commit sin. When Paul prayed for deliverance from his unwanted trouble, God's answer was, "My grace is sufficient for you, for My strength is made perfect in weakness" (2 Cor. 12:9).

In another place, Paul taught the Corinthians, "No temptation has overtaken you except such as is common to man; but God is faithful, who will not allow you to be tempted beyond what you are able, but with the temptation will also make the way of escape, that you may be able to bear it" (1 Cor. 10:13).

The promise of God, then, is that He will never allow His people to suffer under any burden or temptation too great for us to endure. In every instance He will give us His grace, and His grace will be sufficient for us. In the end, His great power will be perfected in our weaknesses.

On the basis of these promises of God, therefore, we may say that the difficulties of adjustment to singleness are basically no different from any other difficulties people may have to confront. They may seem terrible and insufferable, but they are not so severe that you cannot contend with them successfully because "God is faithful . . . [and] will not allow you to be tempted beyond what you are able." His grace will be sufficient for you.

In this sense, then, the so-called gift of singleness is available to any and all who will commit their way to God in faith. Anyone may live as a single person and discover that God is able to provide the daily strength needed to face the special struggles of the single life. This is true even for those whose personal preference would be to marry.

People-do not discover whether or not they possess this thing called the gift of singleness by merely searching the heart's preferences and desires. Instead they must turn to God for His instructions and for the grace to deal with the realities of life.

I may have the desire to be married, but if the reality is that I am single, I have the clear instruction of God's Word telling me I must be celibate. In addition, I also have the promise of God that He will give me what I need to live as a single person. I may, therefore, be assured that I will have the gift of singleness as long as I need it.

This last thought needs to be underscored. The gift of singleness can be either a temporary grace from God or a lifelong calling. Some people, the apostle Paul for example, are actually called to live their entire lives as single persons to better serve the Lord. Through the history of the church, many have actually taken vows of celibacy, thus promising to live unmarried and abstain from sexual activity.

But living as a single person may be only a temporary thing. That, as it turned out, was the case in my life. After I lived alone for fourteen years (and learned to enjoy it very much, I should add), God led Reidun and me to a point at which we knew we ought to marry. We did not marry because we were lacking the gift of singleness but because God had, in His perfect timing, brought us to the decision together.

So, then, what about you? Do you have the gift of singleness? If you are single at this present time, God can give you the gift of His grace. That grace will be sufficient to enable you to live in a strong, positive, and obedient way. If you ask God for that grace, you will receive everything that you need to cope with difficulties (and this certainly includes sexual temptations). His power will live in your weakness and make you strong.

Possessing the grace to live happily as a single person, however, does not necessarily mean that you must always live single. No one can see the future. God may, in time, open the door for you to marry again. There is nothing wrong with a single person desiring to be married.

It would be wrong, though, to desire marriage so intensely or urgently that you are unable to live happily with your singleness. The future is in God's hands. When He is ready, He will reveal to you what He wants you to know. For now, if you are single, your business is to learn to the best of your ability how to make the most of your singleness, including the responsibility of a celibate life. Not all single people are given the *life-calling to celibacy,* but all single people are called to the *responsibility of celibacy.*

Living as a single person may be an exciting, adventurous time of growth. If you embrace your singleness (celibacy and all) and determine to learn and grow and mature, you may soon find that you are becoming a happier and more productive person than you have ever been before. Many others just like you have discovered that this is so.[1]

Earlier, I said that the single person who is willing to accept the rule of God has great potential for the development of sexual fulfillment. This may sound like a very strange thing to say when I have just argued for a celibate life-style. But I sincerely believe it is true because I know that sexual fulfillment is found more in the development of responsible and loving personal relationships than in physical sexual intimacy.

I have learned through personal experience and through counseling with others that an overall sense of sexual fulfillment can never be created by physical sexual activity alone (no matter how pleasant that activity may be). There is also a spiritual dimension to our sexuality that must be more fully developed if we are to become sexually fulfilled persons. In the next three chapters, then, we will look at the nature of love and how it relates to sexual growth and fulfillment.

1. For a very thorough treatment of the choice of a celibate life-style I enthusiastically recommend *Sex and the Single Christian* by Audrey Beslow (Nashville: Abingdon Press, 1987). I have seen nothing better on the subject than this book.

7

Searching for Love's Meaning

There is a popular old song about a fellow who got drunk and proposed to an ugly girl only to wake up terrified that he might end up at the altar with her. The song includes the moral lesson that if you say "I love you" you should be sure it's true because "it's a sin to tell a lie."

The problem for many people is that they don't know how to tell. How, in fact, can you know that you love? For that matter, what is love? Does anybody really know? Aren't there many kinds of love?

Probably the most confused person I ever met sat in my office one day talking about his "love life." His conversation illustrates the widespread uncertainty about the meaning of love.

"Jeff," I asked, "do you think you are in love with Sandy?"

"I don't really know," he said. "I mean, yeah, I love her, sure. It's just that I don't know if that means real love."

"Well," I said, "what do you mean by real love?"

"I don't know. I guess I mean the kind where you really stay together or something. You know, like when you don't get tired of each other."

"So you think real love would always last?" I asked.

"Well, yeah, I guess so. I mean, isn't that right? That's what you always hear."

"But what about Sandy?" I continued. "Are you saying that you are afraid this won't last?"

"Well, how can you ever be sure of that kind of thing? You know, so much can go wrong. You never really know, do you?"

"Tell me what reasons you have to think that maybe you do love Sandy," I said.

"When I'm with her, I really feel great. It's like nothing I've ever felt before in my life."

"Do you mean when you're in bed with her?"

"Right," he paused and looked deep in thought, "it's just really good with her."

"And it was never this good before, with anyone else?" I asked.

"No," he said.

"I wonder why not?" I inquired. "What is different this time?"

"Well, always before, you know, with other women, it was like just as soon as you started making love, they would always seem to get real demanding."

"Tell me about that," I asked.

"Controlling. That's it. Like they wanted to run your life. Like they owned you. I never understand that. Why is it that a woman always seems to think that if you make love to her, that's supposed to mean that you belong to her?"

"I don't know," I said. "But what do you want them to think when you 'make love' to them?"

This question stalled him. He looked at me intently, then stared at the floor a moment and finally said, "I guess I just want them to love me, you know."

"Wait a minute," I said. "That's not what I asked you. I asked you what you want a woman to think you mean when you 'make love' to her."

"I don't know," he said. "It's really hard to answer that. It's hard to understand women."

"Jeff," I said, "I'm not asking you about understanding women. I'm asking you about understanding yourself. What do you mean when you 'make love' to a woman? What do you intend for her to think that means? Does it mean you love her? You call it 'making love.' Is it love? Can she assume that it means love?"

"It always feels like love when I'm doing it," he said.

"But afterward," I said.

"Afterward I get real unsure. I'm always afraid that they'll think it means more than it means."

"Well, Jeff," I asked, "what do you tell them it means? Do you ever say that you love them?"

"Oh, sure, I guess I do. You know, when you're into sex, you'll say things like that."

"Like what?"

"Like, I love you," he spoke sharply. He was frustrated.

"OK. Let me get this straight," I said. "Sometimes, usually I guess, when you're having a sexual relationship with a woman, you will probably say the words 'I love you,' right?"

"Right."

"But you don't necessarily want her to think that means you love her. I mean like really love her?"

"No, because I don't know if I love her that way." He was plainly upset by now.

"So, then, back to my other question. What do you mean when you take a woman to bed and tell her you love her? What is she supposed to think you mean?"

"I want her to think that I like her a lot and that I'm really having a good time," he said.

"So, why not just say that?" I asked. "Why not just say you like her a lot and you're having a good time?"

"No, it just wouldn't seem the same," he said.

"So it feels better to say, 'I love you,' even if you're not sure you really love her?"

"I don't know. I'm really confused about this. You make it all sound cheap."

"Jeff," I said, "I'm only trying to understand you and help you understand yourself. Let me ask you about one thing you said."

"Go ahead," he said.

"Earlier you told me that with Sandy it really seems different. How is it different? Why is it better?"

"Well, she really doesn't seem to be like the others. I mean, she doesn't seem to expect anything but sex."

"You mean she's not demanding. She doesn't act like she owns you or anything," I surmised.

"That's right," he said. "With Sandy it's really free. It's the way I think loving should be."

"No strings," I responded.

"Right," he said.

"So, do you love Sandy?" I inquired.

"You know, I think I do," he said, "but one thing kind of bothers me."

"What's that?" I asked.

"Sandy never says that she loves me."

As I drove home that night I remember having mixed feelings toward Jeff. In a certain way I was just plain angry. He wanted to be loved, but with no strings. He used sex to get close to women so that he could feel loved. Yet he did not want any commitments or promises. Still, he could not risk calling his sexual adventures by any name other than "love." He didn't want it to sound "cheap." *A classic user of women,* I thought.

On the other hand, my heart went out to the obviously tender and gentle fellow who was so insecure about himself, so unsure that he could "really" love. He was entirely without any meaningful definition of love. He had no way to know if he actually loved a woman or if a woman loved him. He knew only about the good feelings of sex, the sensation of being loved, the pleasing sound of the word *love.* But he was afraid and alone.

What is love? How can you know when you are in a love relationship? What are the different ways in which you can love? How can you tell which kind you are experiencing? What does it mean to be "in love"?

All of these questions weave twisting paths through our hearts and minds as we seek to understand ourselves in our relationships with others. And all the questions about love are in one way or another related to our understanding of sexuality. When is love sexual? When is it something else? Is it possible to have a sexual friendship without romance? How can a person know if a friendship is becoming more than a friendship?

How can I be sure it's true when I say, "I love you"? More important, how can I know what I mean when I say, "I love you"?

The Meaning of Love

In the English language the word *love* means many different things. We use the same word to describe our enjoyment of the weather, a good meal, a beautiful place, a wiggly puppy, or a meaningful relationship. Even in personal relationships we use one word to describe various types of relationships.

In discussing love, therefore, we need a careful definition of its meaning. Without clear thinking about our definition of love, we will not know what we mean when we say, "I love you." And we will not know what others mean when they say, "I love you."

For example, if I walk up to a total stranger and say, "I love you," she is very likely to slap my face. And she would be justified in her reaction. She would interpret me as being rude and disrespectful. I have no right to use such a broad term so freely.

If I protest that I meant only "love" in the universal sense of wishing well upon all peoples of the earth, the woman would no doubt respond that I should have said *that* rather than a simple, bold, and undefined "I love you."

In many cases our familiar life context will provide the definition of love for us without much need for explanation. I may say, "I love you," to my wife, my mother or father, my brother or sister, my children or grand-children, or a lifelong friend without feeling the need for definition. Yet in each relationship there is a different shade of meaning for the word *love*.

In newer and less certain relationships, however, *love* may not be used without creating the need for definition. I always remember the first time I told the woman who is now my wife that I loved her. We were only friends at the time, but were growing in our interest for each other. When I said that I loved her, she looked at me rather firmly and said, "You mean as a Christian friend?"

That was exactly what I meant, but I realized at once that I had not clearly conveyed what I meant and that I had somewhat upset and con-fused her. Good for her! She required me to define my meaning so that both of us would be certain about the terms of our relationship.

Suppose, however, that she had not asked me for a definition, but had simply replied that she loved me, too. Then where would we have been? She and I would have gone our separate ways wondering what had just happened. I might have meant only friendship, but she might have taken me to mean far more. Or suppose that I had meant I wanted a more inti-mate and sexual relationship with her, but she understood me to be talking about friendship. Misunderstanding would have been unavoidable.

It is critically important in all human relationships that we know what we mean to each other. Great confusion and pain are frequently caused by our inability to say what we mean and mean what we say. And nowhere is there a greater culprit than this word *love*. We simply must know what it means when we use it.

Love Is a Commandment

The most important thing to learn about love is that God commands it. When the Lord Jesus was asked which of the commandments was the greatest, He replied, "'You shall love the LORD your God with all your heart, with all your soul, and with all your mind.' This is the first and great commandment. And the second is like it: 'You shall love your neighbor as yourself'" (Matt. 22:37–39).

Later, Jesus pointedly directed His disciples to live a life of love: "As the Father loved Me, I also have loved you; abide in My love. If you keep My commandments, you will abide in My love" (John 15:9–10). Then, in a statement that seems to summarize all Christian duty, Jesus added, "These things I command you, that you love one another" (John 15:17).

When we comprehend that love is a commandment, certain truths follow logically. I can think of three that will be very helpful to us as we seek to understand the meaning of love in our lives: (1) love is a moral requirement, (2) love is an act of the will, and (3) love is not determined by feelings.

Love Is a Moral Requirement

If God commands love, we are morally accountable to learn what He means by love and then to discover the means by which we can do the deeds of love. Therefore, learning to love as God requires becomes life's highest goal for those of us serious about meeting our responsibility.

Also, if God has commanded love, it is our highest duty even if others choose not to love. We may not escape our own responsibilities before God just because other people avoid theirs.

Furthermore, the moral requirement of love means that we must focus on learning to love instead of figuring out how to get others to love us. Much of what we think of as love is often no more than a thinly veiled effort to manipulate the responses of other people so that we get what we want. But the duty of love requires us to think not only of ourselves but also of others.

Love Is an Act of the Will

It follows that if love is a commandment, a moral imperative from God, love is an act of the will. Love is something that we may choose to do and then discipline ourselves to continue to do. It would make no sense at all for God to command us to do something we could not command ourselves to do.

For example, I may choose to treat other people with regard and respect even though I do not know them and have no personal interest in them. Simple courtesy to a total stranger is an act of love. I may patiently wait for an elderly woman to go up the stairs and out the door while my personal need is to hurry ahead of her and crowd her out of my way. I may choose what is good for her instead of what is preferable to me. Love has to do with *choosing what is right to do* rather than doing what I may feel like doing.

Love Is Not Determined by Feelings

We get into a lot of trouble because we do not know the difference between love and positive feelings, or emotions. But if love is an act of the will that can be commanded and directed by self-discipline, it cannot be a feeling because we cannot command feelings.

Try it sometime. It is impossible to command what you feel. You may argue with your feelings, but you cannot give them orders. You cannot just stop feeling anger because you decide to stop. You cannot feel happy just because you wish you could. You cannot decide to feel safe and secure when you are filled with anxiety, no matter how hard you try.

Feelings are spontaneous and uncontrollable. They arise from within our deepest perceptions of ourselves and the world around us without the exercise of our wills and often without our approval. Our feelings may be a great embarrassment to us because we do not like feeling what we feel or do not think we *should* feel what we feel.

Feelings come and go. Feelings rise and fall. Feelings change. Therefore, feelings cannot be trusted to guide us in our decisions. When we allow ourselves to be led by our feelings, we are often led into actions that we later regret, even for life. We respect persons who can rise above their feelings in times of decision. We honor those who do what is right to do even though they were afraid or sick or greatly tempted to do evil.

Yet our society persists in thinking that love is primarily something that one feels for another person. This is the constant theme of our "love" songs. I know I love you because of the way I feel. Of course, if my feelings change, I will not love you. But wait a couple of days. Who knows what I might feel then?

It is common for someone in counseling to describe the end of a love relationship in terms of the loss of feelings or the new arousal of feelings in some other direction.

Doug sat across the room from me and summarized his relationship with his wife. "The feeling's gone, Tom. I haven't felt anything for Margie for at least two years now."

"Doug," I replied, "it's a mistake to base your love on how you feel. The more important guide for your relationship with Margie is the fact that she is your wife, and you have made a marriage promise to her. You have to keep that promise and work hard at restoring those pleasant feelings you once had for her."

"It's too late for that now," he said. "There is another woman in my life, and I feel things with her that I never felt with Margie. I'm going to leave Margie and marry Beth."

"But how do you know that your feelings for Beth won't change sometime? How can you know that you won't leave her, too? How can she know that she can trust this 'love' of yours?"

He looked at me long and hard, and finally said, "I don't think you ever can know those things. You just have to go with the feeling you have at the present."

"What is this feeling you have for Beth? Is it love?" I asked.

"If this isn't love, then I don't know what love is," he said with a determined look.

It was my conclusion that Doug was right—he did not know what love is. In two years he had divorced Beth and was asking Margie to consider taking him back.

Great numbers of people are just like Doug. They are hopelessly and helplessly "hooked on a feeling" (apologies to Mac Davis). They believe they are required to follow their feelings no matter what promises they will have to break or what responsibilities they will have to forsake.

A strong wind blowing in our society chants that it is good to follow our feelings no matter where they may lead us. The people who proclaim such things tell us that if the feeling's gone, it is fair play to forsake anything we must (including marriage, of course) to find good feelings again. Better not to live hypocritically. Be honest. Better to find the feeling again. As a people, we are becoming more committed to strong feelings than we are to truth, right, and real love.

It is very easy to see the error in this kind of thinking about love by simply asking, How do I want to be loved? If someone pledges love to me, what do I want that to mean?

Of course, I want good feelings to be in the picture. I want this person to have positive and pleasant emotions. The good feelings often accompanying love relationships are wonderful, and we all hope to have them. But would any of us want that to be the whole picture?

What about those times when the feelings wane and we don't feel so good with each other or about each other? Aren't those the very times when our love has its greatest opportunity to show itself? If someone tells me that I am loved, I hope that it means I am valued and appreciated even (especially) when I am at my worst.

It is, in fact, more likely that I will be assured that I am loved when I am treated with respect and affection although I have been behaving crankily and boorishly. If the person who loves me hangs in there with me even though I am being a pain in the neck, I have some assurance that this is a real love. But if the love offered to me depends entirely on my ability to constantly stir up marvelous feelings of excitement and desire in the breast of my "lover," I would soon doubt that I am loved. (By the way, *lover* as used in this book doesn't necessarily imply a physical sexual relationship. Unfortunately, society has more often than not attached that meaning to the word.)

I should apply the same measurement to myself as I look at my "love" for others. When I say that I love, does that mean I will hang in there? Does it mean that I have made a true commitment of myself to be there for someone else even when cranky and boorish behavior prevails?

Or is my "love" only a good feeling? If it is, it is something other than love. It may be a marvelous, even overwhelming, sensation. But it is a feeling. I cannot command and direct it with my will. Love cannot be like that.

8

Saying
"I Love
You"

I n seeking to understand the meaning of love, we can learn a lot by exploring four ancient Greek words, each of which may be translated "love" in English. They can provide a framework for understanding what we mean when we think of love and when we actually use the word.[1]

Storge

The first Greek word we should consider is *storge* (pronounced storkay), which refers to the enjoyment of familiar things. It is used especially to speak of "family love." But more than that, it involves pleasant associations, tastes, and personal preferences. A variety of things, places, or activities can create a strong sense of affection and attachment.

We can easily say that we "love" ice cream or strawberries. The obvious meaning is that we derive great personal enjoyment from them. In the same way, we will say that we "love" our hometown, an old coat, a walk in the rain, or a cozy fire on a cold winter's night.

In all these instances we are saying only that we enjoy something. More accurately, we are saying that we *enjoy our own feelings* when we possess or experience these things. In short, we are saying that we love feeling this way or that.

However, we may use the word *love* in reference to a relationship with a person but have no deeper meaning than storge. I may say, "I love you," but mean only "I love the way I feel when I'm with you." Such a "love" would be entirely self-centered and based only on personal pleasure and enjoyment. It would not necessarily include any sense of a personal commitment of oneself to responsible behavior toward the other person.

This is what I like to call cat love. Did you ever have a cat rub against your leg? That old cat rubbed one direction and then turned and rubbed the other direction in apparent expression of great devotion. You might have said, "That cat sure does love me."

I think it is far more likely that the cat loves rubbing. He may not rub on anyone else but you because you're all he's got or because you feed him most regularly. But there is no likelihood that the cat has any sense of personal commitment to you or your well-being. He does not understand your moods or care about your hurts. He enjoys what you can give him. And that's that.

If that is all "love" is between humans, we are no better than the animals. If all we "love" is what feels good and pleasing, we love only ourselves and our own pleasure.

On the other hand, we may feel a lot of "love" for our pets. Let's say you have a dog. Every time you come home that dog leaps and barks and runs around in circles and behaves as if he had totally lost his mind just because you appear. You like that, don't you? Sure, you do. Wouldn't it be neat if your spouse and children loved you that much? Your very presence would make them go out of their minds with sheer delight. No wonder you love that dog.

But why do you love the dog? Isn't it because the dog makes you feel good? He faithfully waits for you all day long, he comes when you call, he obeys when you tell him to go away, and he leaves you alone until you call him back. You can even leave him on a chain all day long, and he will still be happy to see you when you return. Pretty neat, huh? Well, try that with a spouse and see how far it gets you.

You see, it's entirely possible that we may say we "love" when all we are really talking about is our great love of our own pleasures and the things in which we find pleasure. It is very revealing to think about our relationships with others in these terms. Far too often, we have what we consider to be love relationships, but actually they are relationships based on personal pleasure.

We might have a much healthier society if we learned to say, "I enjoy you," or "I enjoy the feelings I have when you treat me this way." Such expressions would be much more honest and safe than saying, "I love you." Of course, if we often said, "I enjoy the feelings I have when you treat me this way," we would probably have a much harder time developing relationships. People want more than the knowledge that they are creating good feelings in others. They want to be *loved,* and that means something more than merely being enjoyed.

Eros

The second Greek word for love is *eros* (pronounced air-ose), which refers to sexual passion. In English a number of terms grow out of this word. We speak of erotic books or films or, simply, erotic pleasure. Eros may include various nuances of meaning, but it has two primary characteristics: it is love for a person considered to be worthy, and it is a desire to possess.[2]

Eros-love is closely related to what we often call lust. It is a passion to have something or someone considered attractive. Eros is not necessarily a bad thing, though. It may be a very high and noble form of love if it is combined with honor, trust, and responsibility. Certainly, spouses ought to have eros-love for each other. Remember, an entire book of the Bible is devoted largely to the celebration of eros.

But eros may not be a lot different from storge in one sense. Eros, too, is love of enjoyable feelings. Once again, it is very easy to say, "I love you," when we actually mean, "I love the great feelings your body arouses in my body." Therefore, "I want you."

In modern society there is a great amount of sexual confusion because people easily confuse sexual desire with "true" or "real" love. Therefore, a person may say, "I love you," and be expressing only enjoyment of his own blood pressure and nerve endings.

The Romantic Fallacy

Closely related to the enjoyment of sexual pleasures is the emotional "high" of romance. Romance happens when two people draw close together and believe that they have finally found the "one true love" always intended for them from eternity. It creates a "fairy tale" world for lovers.

This belief is always accompanied by elevated feelings of delight, power, or triumph. People going through such an experience will describe it as a sense that "everything is beautiful," that "all's right with the world," or that "nothing's gonna stop us now." They have found the promised perfect love of which books, songs, and movies are made.

The romance experience is common to all new sexual involvements. It is what we call falling in love, or being in love. Everyone goes through it. And it feels wonderful while it lasts. But it does not last for anyone. Even in the very best love relationships, the romantic euphoria ends.

M. Scott Peck in his wonderful study of love in *The Road Less Traveled* writes,

> The experience of falling in love is invariably temporary. No matter whom we fall in love with, we sooner or later fall out of love if the relationship continues long enough. This is not to say that we invariably cease loving the person with whom we fell in love. But it is to say that the feeling of ecstatic lovingness that characterizes the experience of falling in love always passes. The honeymoon always ends. The bloom of romance always fades.[3]

And it is a good thing that it does, for there are basic fallacies in the romance experience.

In at least four ways the romance experience can be dangerous for people who seriously want to build a strong and lasting love relationship.

1. Love is an overwhelming feeling that comes upon us. The fallacy of romance begins with this entirely false concept of "love." According to this idea, love is something that just happens. It is not something you *will* to happen—it just sort of shoots out of the blue sky and zaps you. It is all emotion, all rush of feeling, and it is entirely uncontrollable. When one is smitten by it, one is helpless.

Now, such a thing happens when we initially "fall for" someone. It does, indeed, seem to drop upon us from the blue sky above. Often, we were not looking for such an experience. In fact, we may have reasons to wish that it would go away and leave us alone. This is what most of the love stories and songs are all about.

This feeling is not love. It is not an act of the will. It is entirely spontaneous and cannot be commanded. One cannot choose to have this experience, nor can one choose *not* to have it. One may choose to take actions on the basis of this experience. One may choose to have sexual intercourse, to marry, or to leave one's spouse on the basis of this feeling. Or one may choose to run like crazy. But this great feeling of euphoria is not love.

2. The feeling always makes for perfect endings. The second part of the fallacy of romance is the idea that because we have this remarkable feeling, everything will turn out just right. This is why you cannot talk sense to people "in love." While they are in this state, they cannot get past the feeling long enough to think rationally. When "lovers" are in the grip of "being in love," they just "know" that the feeling is going to last and everything is going to turn out perfectly in the end.

People get into great trouble sometimes because of this part of the fallacy. I have spoken with many who were involved in a relationship with someone they knew was no good for them. And yet they were so emotionally "in love" that they were unable to act on their best judgment. We even write songs about this experience. *Beware, my foolish heart.* Don't laugh! Some of you have had foolish hearts.

The point is that the emotional euphoria of "being in love" is never capable of producing a happy ending. We must never make a decision that we truly love someone or (especially) that we will marry someone merely because of this feeling. Someday, rest assured, the feeling will be gone— and it may be all that we had.

3. The feeling and the guaranteed perfect ending are created in us by the perfections of the beloved. The third element in the romantic fallacy grows out of our mistaken perception of our "lover's" perfection. We cannot easily see flaws in our lover when we are "in love." If we do see them, we easily ignore them.

We have been relentlessly bombarded by the fairy-tale concept that we will be swept off our feet and carried away to the world of endless dreams with our beloved. The truth is—brace yourself—there are no princes, no Cinderellas, no castles in the sky. We are all just ordinary folks with ordinary warts and character defects. No matter who we fall in love with, sooner or later we will find out that the perfect lover can also be a general nuisance, and many times a great disappointment.

Steve and Brenda had met shortly after Brenda's divorce. They were immediately drawn to each other emotionally and physically. In three months time they had decided to get married. Brenda came to me to ask if I would marry them. When I refused, she became very upset.

"I was afraid you would be like this," she said.

"Brenda," I replied, "you just haven't known each other long enough to decide to get married."

"But Tom," she protested, "Steve is a wonderful man."

"He may well be," I said, "I don't know him. But that's my point,

Brenda. You don't know him either. Right now he is very attractive to you, and he seems to do everything right. But you haven't had enough time to see everything that he is; and he hasn't seen all there is in you either."

Brenda left my office frustrated. In about a month I heard that they had married. About nine months later, she came back to see me.

"I wish I had listened to what you were saying, Tom. Steve has some real problems. He never really wants to stay home at night. He runs around with his buddies all the time. Now he's lost his job and he doesn't seem very motivated to look for another one. He is very jealous of any time I spend with my family. And yet, when we are alone together he isn't attentive. I really don't think we can last very long."

"Do you mean you're thinking about a divorce?" I asked.

"Yes, I guess I am. I just don't think Steve is the right one for me. I thought he was, but . . ."

Steve and Brenda's relationship provides a helpful illustration of one aspect of the romantic fallacy. It is quite possible that a relationship built of this fallacy will not last. Suppose that the relationship fails to deliver. Suppose that it ends.

Well, if it ends, where did the problem lie? What went wrong? If one believes that happy endings are based on the perfections of one's partner, then it becomes quite likely that the partner will be blamed for all failure in the relationship. Obviously, this was *the wrong partner*. This was not a prince, but a mere frog in disguise.

But—notice this—if I believe that my problem was that I had the wrong partner I do not necessarily learn that I had believed a fallacy. I can go right back out looking for Miss Perfect. The fallacy may easily persist in my mind while I go through several partners and never really learn how to build a genuine love relationship.

4. The feeling is spontaneous. We have already said that this feeling, wrongly identified as love, is spontaneous. The real danger is that it leads to the belief that real love is easy. Wrong again. *Real love is hard.* Real love requires work. One reason so many marriages fail is that the individuals did not realize what would be required of them to love. They thought it would be easy. Romance is easy. Love is hard.

Don't get me wrong. I'm not against romance or spontaneity in a genuinely loving relationship. But I believe it is essential to know the difference between romance and love. Romance is based on sexual attraction, the enjoyment of affection, and imagination. Love is based on decisions, promises, and commitments.

Philia

The third Greek word for love that we should consider is *philia* (pronounced phil-eé-ah), which refers to the love of friendship. It is often called brotherly love. Most of us know that the name Philadelphia means just that (from *philia*, love, and *adelphos*, brother). Philia has great breadth of meaning but generally involves some shared interest that draws people together and then bonds them to each other.

Friends love because they share something in common. Initially, they may be drawn to each other because of a mutual love of some activity, such as football or gardening or painting. With the passing of time, however, their friendship grows to include appreciation for each other. Their common interest keeps bringing them back together, in many cases for years and years. In turn, their many times together deepen their ability to enjoy each other.

Phileo-love may be a deeply enriching and broadening experience for two people, or even for a larger group. Certainly it is a higher kind of love than storge or eros. Philia lifts us above mere enjoyment of our feelings to the level of the enjoyment and appreciation of a personal relationship. To a degree, therefore, it truly brings us into the lives of other persons.

Yet philia, like storge and eros, has weaknesses. The fact that it can create a very strong bond between people may sometimes mean that it will not be good for us. It may be harmful at times. For example, our friends are most likely to be blind to our faults. At least, they are most likely to say nothing to us about our faults. More than that, our friends will usually defend us even when we are wrong, and in so doing they may help us feel justified in doing what is wrong.

Leon Morris, in his *Testaments of Love,* writes of how a group of friends may strengthen a person in his weaknesses:

> Friends refuse to be controlled by outside opinion, because this is part of what friendship means. This means that when outsiders are wrong, friends strengthen one another in the right. But it also means that when those outside are right, the friends may well encourage one another to continue in a wrong way. Their very friendship hinders them from seeing what is right in the contention of outsiders. Further, their bond may lead to pride, which despises those not admitted to the intimacy of the circle.[4]

So the essential weakness of storge and eros is found in philia as well. I may say that I love my friend, but mean only that I love the fact that he or she encourages or supports me in those things of mutual interest to us. If my interest (or my friend's) should change, the love may quickly end.

Jim and Don had been friends since high school. Back in those days they had always played golf together. They had also double-dated, and even after they were married, they and their wives would often go out together. But they had little to hold them together but golf and social times with their wives.

When Jim became manager of the company where he worked, he had little time for golf and gradually lost interest in the game. Rather predictably, his friendship with Don slowly ebbed away. They have few contacts with each other now. When they do see each other it is still enjoyable, but it's not the same. Don says, "We were really great friends, but Jim changed."

What had once seemed to be a strong personal bond between these inseparable buddies was later seen to be less than that. The bond between them was not deeply personal; it was a superficial relationship based on mutual enjoyment of golf.

We may easily discover the weakness of this form of love by thinking of how we wish to be loved. Do I wish to be loved only because I share something in common with another? Must I love gardening or football to be loved by this other person? Am I to be loved only because I encourage and strengthen another in what he or she enjoys?

If we define love only in these terms, then, we end up with what amounts to a mere trade. I love you because you love me, and how could I not love someone who loves me? You love what I love and that makes me enjoy you, and vice versa, and that feels good.

The element of mutuality lifts us to a higher level in our understanding of love in that it introduces the importance of sharing ourselves. But mutuality also places a limitation on love. If you will no longer scratch my back, it is not likely that I will scratch yours much longer.

If, then, I say, "I love you," and my meaning is philia, it is still possible that I have not progressed beyond thinking about my personal enjoyment. I enjoy you because you are fun to be with, intellectually stimulating, or just plain comfortable. But if for some reason you cease to be fun for me, or intellectually stimulating, or comfortable, I may soon choose to move on to other people.

Shall we stop here in our search for the meaning of love? Shall we decide that love is only a kind of trade? At first that might sound like a good idea. None of us very much likes the idea of getting into a one-sided relationship with anyone. Who wants to do all the giving while another does all the receiving? Let's be fair about this—love should be a fifty-fifty thing. Right?

Well, maybe and maybe not. I'm not so sure that I want to be loved that way. First of all, I don't think I know how to tell when my friend (or my spouse) and I have reached the point of fifty-fifty. What sort of measurement can be used for that? Perhaps I can know that you paid last time, and that means I should pay this time. Certain objective things can be measured. But how do you go about measuring the intangible parts of a relationship? How do you know that you have given more or cared more or hurt more than the other person?

Second, when I think about being loved this way, I do not feel very secure. If you tell me that you love me, but your meaning is that I must give 50 percent and you will give 50 percent, the relationship seems rather shaky to me. Instead of creating a sense of fairness or balance, this approach seems to create an attitude of caution and guardedness. I would always be watching myself to be sure that I had not loved you too much, and I would be checking up on you to be certain that you had not loved me too little. This is not the love I desire.

1. Leon Morris, *Testaments of Love* (Grand Rapids: William B. Eerdmans, 1981), p. 114.
2. Ibid., p. 120.
3. M. Scott Peck, *The Road Less Traveled* (New York: Simon and Schuster, 1978), p. 84.
4. Morris, *Testaments of Love,* p. 118.

9

Agape: The Love That Is True

The last of the Greek words for love is the one we are looking for. It is *agape* (pronounced a-gah-pay). Agape is familiar to most Christians because this is the special word used almost exclusively by Jesus and the apostles to speak of the love of God for man and the love Christians are commanded to have for others.

Agape was not a common term to express love before the time of the New Testament. It seems to have come into use because Jesus and His followers were teaching a whole new concept of what it meant to love. Familiar words for love, such as eros and philia, probably would have carried with them too many other connotations. A new word was needed.

Originally, agape seems to have meant something like "to prefer." It was not a very emotional word, but conveyed the idea of the making of a free choice. It is easy to see how well the word would carry the concept of the electing love of God. God does not "fall in love" with sinful men and women because He is emotionally attracted to them by some merit they possess. Instead, God freely chooses to treat them in a gracious way entirely because it is His character to do so.

Leon Morris summarizes the meaning of the new word:

Perhaps as good a way as any of grasping the new idea of love the Christians had is to contrast it with the idea conveyed by *eros*. As we have seen, *eros* has two principal characteristics: it is a love of the worthy and it is a love that desires to possess. *Agape* is in contrast at both points: it is not a love of the worthy, and it is not a love that desires to possess. On the contrary, it is a love given quite irrespective of merit, and it is a love that seeks to give.[1]

The love called agape, then, is a love freely chosen. The person who loves with agape-love does not ask if the other person deserves to be loved in such a way. He simply chooses to love that person by an act of his will. In choosing to love with agape-love he does not focus on what he is feeling or needing, nor does he focus on what he expects to gain by loving. Instead, he focuses on the good of the other person. Agape-love looks not at what may be gained but at what may be freely given. Agape-love is *freely chosen* and *freely given*.

The most helpful study of love that I have read is John Powell's book, *The Secret of Staying in Love*. Powell lists seven theses about the nature of love:

1. Love is not a feeling
2. Love is a decision-commitment
3. Effective love is unconditional
4. Love is forever
5. The commitment of love involves decisions
6. The essential gift of love is a sense of personal worth
7. Love means the affirmation, not the possession of the one loved.[2]

Powell's theses are extremely useful in gaining an understanding of agape-love. We have previously considered some of his ideas, such as the fact that love is not a feeling but an act of will. But much more can be learned from his list.

Love Is an Unconditional Commitment

To say that agape-love is unconditional means that it is given entirely without charge. It is not given because the person loved deserves it or has somehow earned it. In fact, if it could be earned, it would not be agape-love. As Dr. Morris said, agape-love is given quite irrespective of merit. This love has no price tag on it. It is a gift with no strings attached, no exception clauses, no small print. I cannot love if I attach conditions to what I call love. Conditions nullify love.

Agape-love lifts us to an entirely new level of thinking about love and love relationships. The other forms of love are basically oriented to what *I* like, what *I* enjoy, or what *I* get in return for loving. But when we love with agape-love, we choose to love others because we believe it is good to do so. We believe it is good for the persons we are loving to be thought of and treated as we have chosen to think of them and treat them. Even if they do not respond positively to our love, even if our love is rejected, we still believe that we should extend our love to them.

Sue Johnson loves Bruce Wilson. Sue teaches ninth-grade algebra. Bruce is her student. For over two months Sue has met with Bruce two evenings per week to give him special tutoring. Sue does not get paid extra for this. In fact, it costs her money because she can't ride in her usual car pool when she meets with Bruce. But Sue is personally committed to Bruce's learning. She has told Bruce and his parents that there is no limit to her willingness to help him. She will keep on meeting with him as often and as long as it takes to bring him to the appropriate level of learning. Sue's love for Bruce is unconditional.

Alice works hard for Mike. She gets up early to fix his lunch and cook his breakfast. She spends many hours during most days caring for his needs. She cooks, sews, launders, irons, and does other chores. She is not paid for her work, nor does she want pay. Sometimes Mike does not express appreciation to her. He seems to take her for granted. She notices, but she continues to do what she can to make Mike's life simpler. She does it because she loves Mike. He is her son, and she loves him unconditionally.

Ed loves Helen. He spends almost all day every day waiting on her needs. He feeds her, cleans up for her, talks to her, changes TV channels for her, and helps her dress. But Helen never does anything for Ed. She has suffered a debilitating stroke, and she will never do anything for Ed again. But Ed is her husband, and he will be faithful and attentive to Helen no matter how hard it gets. He loves her unconditionally.

In each example, love is given with no thought of reward. It is not given for pay or for praise. It is given only because the one giving it wants to give it for the sake of the other. Only the good of the person loved is in view.

At the same time, there is a reward in loving this way. It is the reward of having extended ourselves. When we love because it is right to love, we grow. When we come out of ourselves and give ourselves to others only because they are important, we become more whole. The reward of agape-love is not in gaining something for ourselves, but in giving of ourselves for others' gain.

In the examples of love given above, one party was generally unable to give anything in return. What of relationships between apparently equal partners? Is it really possible to give love unconditionally to someone who is able to respond but does not? John Powell addresses this question:

Can we expect one party in a love relationship to continue making an unconditional contribution and commitment of love without a sustaining response from the other? Theoretically, I believe that if a person could continue offering an unconditional love the other would in time respond. But perhaps it would be too late. If the person trying to offer unconditional love is given nothing in response, to nourish his own capacity and renew his strength for love, the relationship may be brought to an inevitable failure.[3]

Powell goes on to add,

"Unconditional love" should be interpreted as an ideal, a goal towards which true love aspires, but which is realistically not within human reach or attainment. We are all to some extent injured, limited by the throb of our own needs and pains. Only a totally unscarred and free person could consistently give unconditional love. Such a person, of course, does not exist.[4]

I would like to make two responses to Mr. Powell's remarks. First, it is probably true that no mere human being can love in a totally unconditional way. Our scars and pains being what they are, we are all probably too afraid, too suspicious, and too self-centered and self-protecting to extend ourselves in a fully unconditional way for another. In our frail human condition, we will, even at our best, love with limitations.

But when Mr. Powell says that no one is able to give unconditional love consistently, he seems to forget the existence of God. For the Bible attributes unconditional love to God. And that unconditional love, freely given to us through the death of the Lord Jesus Christ, is set before us in the Scriptures as the example and the source of our love in human relationships.

Jesus said, "As the Father loved Me, I also have loved you; abide in My love. . . . love one another as I have loved you. Greater love has no one than this, than to lay down one's life for his friends" (John 15:9, 12–13). It is clear from this and other scriptural passages that those who have received the love of God in Christ are called upon to love in the same way and with the same kind of love that Jesus Christ has given. That love is agape-love, which is unconditional.

It is the idea of agape-love, for example, that underlies Christ's teaching that His followers should love even those who treat them badly.

Love your enemies, do good to those who hate you, bless those who curse you, and pray for those who spitefully use you. . . . And just as you want men to do to you, you also do to them likewise (Luke 6:27–31).

Agape-love was the motivation of Stephen, the first disciple to die for Christ, when he prayed with his dying breath, "Lord, do not charge them with this sin" (Acts 7:60). The same attitude was seen in the apostle Paul's spirit toward those who had failed to support him in a time of trouble. In a letter to his friend Timothy he wrote, "No one stood with me, but all forsook me. May it not be charged against them" (2 Tim. 4:16).

The story has often been told of George Washington Carver, the famous black educator and scientist, who displayed the love of Christ in a remarkable way to an arrogant and thoughtless white man. Carver arrived at a Midwestern hotel where he was to speak at a gathering of scientists and business people. While standing in the hotel lobby he was noticed by a man who had just arrived and was carrying several pieces of luggage.

"Hey, boy," the man called to Carver.

"Are you speaking to me?" Carver asked.

"Yes, you boy, take care of my bags," the man demanded.

Carver picked up the man's bags and took them up the elevator and down the hall to the man's room. All the way he listened to the man's proud description of the latest scientific developments in the world.

Once they had reached the fellow's room, he fumbled in his pocket, produced a quarter, and offered it to Carver.

"Sir, I don't want your money," George Carver said.

Wondering if he had made some kind of mistake, the man asked, "What's your name?"

"My name is Carver," was the reply.

Knowing that he had made a mistake, the man struggled to apologize. "You're George Washington Carver," he said. "Mr. Carver, I'm sorry. I thought. . . ."

"I know what you thought," Carver said.

"But you are one of the most famous men in America right now," the man replied. "Why on earth did you help me with my bags?"

Carver's answer is a remarkable example of agape-love.

"Sir, you needed help."

Carver's ability to look past the offensiveness of this man's style and attitude enabled him to see something that many of us would likely miss at such a time. He saw that the man had too many bags to carry. And he was willing to help. Perhaps the man did not deserve to be treated so kindly, but agape can see that even those who do not deserve love still need it.

Although it may still be said that no mere human being will ever reach unconditional love perfectly, we must, nevertheless, accept the calling God has given us to love with the unconditional love of agape. This means, as Powell has said, that unconditional love must be set before us as the ideal love, the love toward which we must aim our own hearts.

We may not be expected to become perfect in our efforts at unconditional love, but we will grow in our ability to love only as we make Christ our pattern and unconditional love our goal. If we settle for anything less than the goal of unconditional love, we will remain locked inside ourselves. The distinction of unconditional love is that it draws us out of ourselves and enables us to truly give.

One other thing needs to be said about unconditional love. It involves the highest risk that a person can take. By offering myself to you unconditionally, I have made myself totally vulnerable to whatever insult or injury you may wish to give me. You may reject my love, and that is the greatest of all pains. But unconditional love accepts that risk.

The risk of unconditional love is required of persons who marry. Marriage requires of a man and a woman that they be wholly given to each other, wholly vulnerable to each other. And this total givenness is beautifully symbolized in the openness and vulnerability of the sexual union.

For this reason, only those who are willing to grow in their ability to love unconditionally will be able to grow toward sexual fulfillment. Sexual fulfillment demands the abilities to love deeply, to give of oneself, and to become wholly vulnerable to another. In our search for sexual wholeness we must learn to love unconditionally.

Love Requires the Making of Decisions

At the same time love requires the making of decisions. Obviously, I cannot love all people in the same way and to the same degree. There is only one of me, and I do not have the capacity, the time, or the strength to give myself to all in the same way. I must make choices regarding the persons I will love and the specific way I will love. This does not make my love conditional; it makes my love responsible. To promise more than I would be able to give would be to act irresponsibly.

It is clear, therefore, that there are degrees of love within the sphere of agape. For example, agape causes me to stop to help an elderly man retrieve his spilled groceries even though I am in a considerable hurry. It is self-giving, it is focused on the needs of another person, and it is an act of my will. It is based on a general commitment that I have made to be helpful to others in need.

But it takes only a moment of my time and a minimum exertion of energy. I could offer to pick up the man each week, take him to the grocery store, help him with the shopping, and take him back home again. This would still be agape, but the love offered would be greater because the commitment would be greater.

The love we call agape, then, has to do with our ability to make and keep commitments to one another. I am able to measure my love for another person only in terms of *the promises I am willing to make to him*. As my willingness to make deeper and more meaningful commitments to another increases, I may know that my love for him has increased.

On the deepest level agape-love is committed to touching the inner life of another person in such a way as to strengthen and enrich that life. This is what Scott Peck speaks of when he defines love as "the will to extend one's self for the purpose of nurturing one's own or another's spiritual growth."[5] This kind of love requires more of us than any other kind. At this level of love we are interested in the most significant matter of all—the health and growth of another person's inner soul.

To love on this level takes much time and great expense of energy. Therefore, we may love only a few people in this way. To promise such love to more than a select few would be irresponsible, for we would be promising more than we could give. We ordinarily give this love to our families and, perhaps, to a few intimate friends. This love causes us to live for others.

Of course, this aspect of agape-love is implicitly required of marriage partners. And, because the terms of marriage call for complete vulnerability and givenness to each other, they also necessarily exclude all others. The choice to marry one person is automatically the decision to close the door on all others with regard to the special love privileges belonging to marriage.

Sexuality, therefore, includes the potential to make the exclusive decision of marriage. Unmarried persons should view their sexual nature as a very special part of themselves that may one day be given exclusively to a special chosen person. Until the time when marriage is appropriate, unmarried persons need to decide to avoid the sexual involvement that exclusively belongs to marriage. To keep one's sexual nature reserved especially for one's spouse is a high form of agape-love.

At a recent Fresh Start Seminar a woman was explaining to me how she had told a male friend that she would not go to bed with him. She was strongly attracted to him and had begun to be affectionate with him. He was beginning to suggest that they become more physically involved, but she resisted.

When he asked for an explanation, here is what she said: "I know that you care about me, and even think that you love me. In some ways, I think I love you. But you are asking me to do something I believe only married people have the right to do. You and I haven't even defined the nature of our relationship yet, so how can we allow ourselves such powerful expressions? I think the best way to show that we love each other right now is by self-control.

"There's something else I want to say to you. Since we cannot know that we will ever get married to each other, we need to realize that there could be two other people in this picture. You may have a wife someday, and I may have a husband. I don't know who your wife will be, but whether it's me or some other woman, I want you to learn whatever you learn about sex with her. I will not steal that from her. It's too precious. I hope that you will feel the same way toward me and my husband."

This woman had made an agape-love decision. She was thinking of the exclusive nature of married love. She did not want to give to any man what she knew was the exclusive right of her husband. To use the language of a former generation, she was "keeping herself" for marriage. Not bad language, actually.

Furthermore, she was also exercising agape-love toward her friend and whoever might one day become his wife. She was unwilling to defile what belonged to them alone. Agape-love knows that marriage requires an exclusive commitment. Therefore, agape must make exclusive decisions regarding sexual behavior, even before marriage.

Love Is Forever

Also, love is forever. This is just another way of saying that love is unconditional. It means that love is not conditioned upon the changes that may come with time. This characteristic of love usually gives us the greatest test because it emphasizes that no matter what happens, a love commitment may not be taken back. If I offer to love you only up to a certain point, I have not offered to love you at all. Love must be what Powell calls a life-wager.[6]

As noted earlier, if I truly give the gift of love to another person, I take the risk of allowing that person to reject my love. Powell writes,

> My decision must never in any way preempt your freedom. I must be me and offer my gift, but at the same time I must let you be you, free to accept or to reject my gift. This is perhaps the most difficult line that true love must walk, being myself and offering my contributions according to my lights and yet never forcing your acceptance or response.[7]

Perhaps this aspect of agape-love shows us most clearly whether or not we truly possess it. In the final analysis, my willingness to extend myself to another means very little if I will do so only when I am safe. True love must always take the risk of being rejected.

Many who go through a divorce face a special problem with unconditional-forever love. The question is, How can I go on loving when my love has been totally rejected? To answer this question, it is important to remember the difference between one's personal decision to love and the growth of a love relationship.

One person may make a genuine commitment of unconditional-forever love to another person, but one person does not have the power to automatically guarantee the successful growth of a relationship. The development of a lasting love relationship takes two committed persons. Sadly, there are times when a marriage must end because one partner chooses to forsake the marriage covenant completely. In such cases it is impossible for the force of the forsaken partner's commitment to magically heal the marriage.

When my marriage ended, I struggled long and hard with this issue. How could I give up on the marriage, even though my wife had plainly brought it to an end? Wasn't my pledge of love to her a lifetime pledge? Wasn't I committed to love forever, no matter what she did? How could I accept the end of the marriage without breaking my own vow of committed love?

The answer to those questions came in two parts. First, I had to learn that there is nothing love can do to force other people to keep their commitments. That is not the point of love. In fact, love always recognizes that the other person has the freedom to refuse or reject the love offered. And it is the nature of love to take that risk.

Second, I had to learn that even though a genuine commitment may not be withdrawn, it is necessary to accept the changes created by a complete rejection. Furthermore, when one recognizes and accepts the reality that one's partner has permanently ended the relationship, it then becomes necessary to redefine and adjust the terms of one's love commitment.

A special quality of agape-love is its ability to offer genuine love, despite rejection, abandonment, or betrayal, and at the same time to recognize the changes in the nature of the relationship that are required. In the exercise of this special quality a forsaken spouse may accept the end of the marital love commitment and continue to offer love to the former spouse, not as a spouse, but as a person. The special quality is forgiveness.

Love Is Willing to Forgive

To love unconditionally and forever implies willingness to forgive. If I truly love you, I will take the risk of making myself vulnerable to the injury you could give me by abusing or rejecting my love. I cannot force you to receive or return my love. I am able only to offer my love genuinely, and to do so means that I will forgive you if you mistreat me or reject me. That is, I will not allow your rejection of my love to bring my love to an end.

All human relationships require the element of forgiveness to continue and to grow. People being what they are, failure and weakness will be present in every relationship. Agape-love includes the willingness to keep loving even though the loved one is not at all times lovable. Each of us needs to be loved in this way, and we need to learn to love forgivingly.

But people do not easily accept the idea of making open-ended commitments to forgive. To many people this sounds like total stupidity. But why does it sound so stupid? Isn't it because we are still thinking about ourselves? Isn't it because we are still placing limits on our love? Isn't it because we are saying that we will extend ourselves *only so far* for others? Isn't it because we are still loving conditionally?

To love with unconditional and ongoing forgiveness means that *love affirms the worth of the one loved*. When I truly love, I am saying that I believe you are someone of personal worth. You may not return my love. You may actually spurn my love or even treat me with great disrespect. You may abandon me completely. But you are still someone of worth, still someone whose life I should affirm. To love in this way means that I will love you even when you are at your worst (perhaps, especially when you are at your worst), for then you most need the affirmation of my love.

Many years ago I was given this kind of affirmation when a personal failure had put me in a position of shame and embarrassment. Many people had lost their confidence in me, and the future of my ministry was seriously in doubt. I was feeling alone and entirely unworthy. At that time a friend of mine brought me great affirmation. I will always remember his words.

He said, "Tom, I can't imagine being more disappointed or let down. I think this is the most pain and embarrassment I have ever felt. But I'm sure you feel it more than I do. And I want you to know that even though I am deeply disappointed, I still believe in you. And I will always be your friend."

I felt as if a dark cloud had lifted after he said that. He was telling me that even though I had failed him and hurt him, he was willing to reach beyond the pain I had caused to embrace me. In effect, he was saying that I was still worth the investment of his time and energy. He still valued me, and he would never let our friendship end. He showed me the love called agape, which forgives and affirms.

Undoubtedly the greatest example of forgiving love was that given by Jesus Christ when He was on the cross. While the soldiers crucified Him and gambled for His clothing, Jesus prayed, "Father, forgive them, for they do not know what they do" (Luke 23:34).

What shall we say about Jesus' attitude toward His killers? That He was foolish? That He was passive or weak? Indeed not! The Scriptures make it abundantly plain that Jesus *chose* to be there on that cross for the sake of His murderers and many others like them because He loved them.

John, the apostle, saw in the death of Christ the greatest of all definitions of agape-love: "By this we know love, because He laid down His life for us. And we also ought to lay down our lives for the brethren" (1 John 3:16).

Here is love at its highest. The total giving of the Savior is set before us as the one thing that will show us what agape-love is. To love is to give of ourselves to the end, no matter how much pain we must endure. This is the way we, too, ought to live. We ought to lay down our lives for our brothers because they are persons of great worth. Even if they reject our love to the end, we must never close our hearts to them.

Agape-love accepts the pain that comes in valuing others. When someone hurts me, I have two choices. I can choose to protect myself from the pain by abandoning the one who has hurt me. Or I can choose to embrace the person and the pain. That was exactly what Jesus did on the cross. He embraced the pain caused by humans because His only other option was to let mankind go. Rather than let us go, He willingly took our pain unto Himself.

It may be especially helpful to persons who have been betrayed by a spouse to remember the words of Jesus on the cross. In His unwavering love He actually prayed that the Father would forgive those who were putting Him to death. "Forgive them," He said, "for they do not know what they do." Forgiving love is able to look beneath the surface and see the confusion of the other person's life.

On many occasions I have used Christ's remark in our Fresh Start ministry. In urging people to forgive their ex-mates I have asked them to look deeply at that person's inner life. What have been the circumstances of the spouse's life? What things have caused him (her) to become the kind of person he (she) is today? What was lacking in that person's childhood development? Is it not possible to look at that ex-spouse and say, "He (She) does not know what he (she) is doing"? Is it not possible to look beneath the surface and see someone who, in spite of his (her) present behavior, still needs to be loved and forgiven?

One woman with whom I talked said it best: "My husband never had a chance. He was born rich, an only child. He was spoiled by his family as far as money and privileges were concerned. But he never had any kind of real love from his parents. His mother farmed him out to others constantly so that she could play the socialite scene. And his father never had any time for him. More than that, his father was repeatedly involved in affairs with other women. He grew up seeing his father play around and his mother quietly permit it. He is just a child who never really had a chance to learn how to love anybody. If only someone could help him."

With compassion and forgiveness she was realistically evaluating the man she had married. She knew her marriage was finished. She had no unrealistic desires to have him back. She knew that it would be foolish to take him back. Still, her heart could feel deeply for him, for his needs, for his pain and confusion that had warped his life. She could no longer love him as a wife, but she could see his worth as a person. And she could forgive.

Love Does Not Mean the Sacrifice of the Self or the Loss of Personal Integrity

Agape-love does not mean the sacrifice of the self or the loss of personal integrity. The thought of unconditional, total self-giving is often misunderstood to mean that we ought to "give up" or "give away" our lives. Sometimes what is called Christian love has been wrongly understood to mean a kind of weak and passive "niceness" that always yields to what others want. After all, doesn't the Bible teach us to "deny ourselves," to "turn the other cheek," and to "return good for evil"? Because of an unbalanced interpretation of such passages, some people believe that it is "loving" to passively stand by while the ones they "love" misbehave terribly.

In some instances this view of love has led people into complete passivity and total loss of self-respect. We can all think of examples of people who, out of a misguided understanding of love, actually contribute to the misbehavior of others. Some parents "love" their children too much to correct them or to require them to accept responsibility. Actually, such parents are not acting lovingly because they are not giving their children what they truly need. By failing to correct bad behavior, these parents are unwittingly training their children to believe that bad behavior is acceptable.

Another common example of this kind of thinking is evident in the wife who believes that "love" requires her to allow her husband to treat her any way he pleases, even if he is abusive or unfaithful. Dr. James Dobson has written an entire book, *Love Must Be Tough*, dealing with the problem of wives who discover that their husbands are having affairs but do nothing to resist or correct the situation. Dr. Dobson insists that real love must always require responsibility from those who are loved.[8]

Real agape-love calls me to give myself totally and unconditionally, but agape-love never asks me to give away my self-respect or integrity. To truly love you, I must give of my very best, which requires me to maintain my self-respect and integrity. If I allow you to mistreat me and I do not protest, I have not loved you, for it is not good for you to mistreat others. Nor am I being good to you when I fail to tell you that your behavior is wrong. If I am truly devoted to your well-being, I must face you with my integrity when I know that you have been wrong.

That surely does not mean I should become your critic or judge in a negative sense. Neither does it mean I should become impatient or unforgiving with you. If I truly love you, I will forgive you seventy times seven times. I will hang in there with you because you are of infinite value to me. But I will hang in there with all the strength of my integrity.

To love with integrity means that I will tell you the truth, even when the truth may be painful for me to tell and for you to hear. I will not be unforgiving or self-righteous in telling the truth, but I will insist on the truth for your sake. To do anything less would be to fail to love you because it would mean that I had not given you my very best.

The commitment to love with integrity is never higher or more demanding than in marriage; two people commit themselves to each other in a lifelong pursuit of knowing and loving with integrity. The marriage commitment says, "I will never give you anything but my best. I will be as true and honest as I know how to be, always and ever. I will give you my forgiveness, no matter what that requires of me. But I will always insist that you grow into the best person you can be. I will want the best for you, expect the best from you, and give myself to help you achieve the best."

Scott Peck calls this kind of love "judicious giving":

> Love is not simply giving; it is *judicious* giving and judicious withholding as well. It is judicious praising and judicious criticizing. It is judicious arguing, struggling, confronting, urging, pushing and pulling in addition to comforting. It is leadership. The word "judicious" means requiring judgment, and judgment requires more than instinct; it requires thoughtful and often painful decision-making.[9]

To love judiciously, then, means both to accept others as they are and, also, to be fully committed to their growth. Healthy parents love their child this way. Loving parents hold these two parts of love in full view at all times. They love their child unconditionally. Before the child is grown, they will have forgiven him a multitude of sins. They will never stop forgiving their child because their love is true.

But the love of these forgiving parents will also constantly guide, correct, and discipline the child. Parents who love their child are fully committed to doing whatever it takes to guide the child to mature and responsible adulthood. Because they love, they will discipline the child. That is, they will teach and correct the child, which will be hard and often frustrating work. But love requires it. Love, you see, is hard work.

When Al and Mary discovered that their son Kevin was taking drugs, they confronted him strongly. At first, Kevin denied that he was on drugs, but his parents had uncovered too much evidence for him to maintain his lies. Finally, he admitted that he was taking "some stuff" but argued that it was harmless and that he knew what he was doing. When his parents responded with stricter rules, Kevin reacted with greater rebellion. Things came to a head one night when Al followed Kevin to a drug party and forcibly took him back home. The conflict erupted into a long and emotional battle in which a lot of regrettable things were said.

After that night Al and Mary worked hard at staying in close touch with Kevin daily. They required him to talk with a police drug counselor as well as with the pastor of their church. Once every week they had a family meeting in which they would discuss whatever subject Kevin wanted. They maintained a firm control and discipline over Kevin's life, yet constantly affirmed their love for him. Once a week they planned some kind of family activity for just the three of them.

Kevin did not respond well at first, but after several months he began to recognize that his parents' commitment to him was very deep. He could see that the parents of some of his friends were in no way willing to be so involved with their children. He didn't agree with his parents about some things, but he learned that their love for him had no limit. Al and Mary loved with integrity.

The same kind of "hard love" is required of spouses, but with a major difference. In marriage, there are presumably two mature adults. As a matter of fact, many who marry are not yet fully grown up (not even if they are in their thirties or forties). But persons who marry usually think they are grown up and generally resent the efforts of other persons to correct them. They do not wish to be treated "like children."

This rather natural resentment toward the corrective efforts of others often causes problems in marriage. Not long after the emotional high of the honeymoon, most couples settle into a fairly mundane and ordinary routine. Everyday pressures and problems cause them to see each other in new ways. Soon there are disagreements and conflict. The efforts at correction begin, and the result can be strong argument, stubborn resistance, and heartache. Soon, they may be asking, "Where did the love go?"

When Ben and Shirley first got married, they thought their love was perfect. They got along so well for the first year that it was a great shock to them when they began to struggle in their relationship. When they went to see the marriage counselor, they were uncertain what had gone wrong or who was to be blamed.

"There really isn't any one thing that I can put my finger on," Shirley told the counselor. "It just seems that Ben isn't as attentive as he used to be. Sometimes I don't think he likes me very much."

"Of course I like you, Shirley," Ben said, "I love you. It's just hard to show you that when you're always on me about something."

"What kind of things do you mean, Ben?" the counselor asked.

"Oh, little things," Ben said, "like, I can't come home and throw my coat on the chair. I have to hang it up the minute I walk in the door or else she's all over me."

"Is that right, Shirley?"

"Yes, I do want him to hang his coat up. Is that so much to ask? I work hard to make our home neat and clean, and I think that the least he can do is not make a mess with his clothes. It doesn't take any more effort to hang his coat up than it does to toss it on some chair. I wish he'd take a little pride in our home."

"Why do you think Shirley is unreasonable, Ben?" the counselor asked. "I can understand her desire to keep the house neat."

"I understand it, too," Ben said. "I want a neat house just like she does."

"Then what's the problem?" the counselor asked.

"Sometimes I feel like I'm still a little boy back home with my mother," Ben said. "I feel that if Shirley really loved me she could accept me the way I am."

Ben and Shirley are a good example of people who make the mistake of assuming that efforts at correction are unloving. But it is precisely in the midst of these struggles that agape-love has its greatest opportunity. These are the very things that love must deal with through the whole course of a marriage if the relationship is going to grow in a healthy way. It is in the mutual commitment to what Scott Peck called "judicious giving and judicious withholding" that a couple will grow in love.

That is not what the movies show us and the love songs idealize, though. For that reason many people go through their entire courtship primarily focused on romantic fantasies and physical sexuality, dreaming about how perfect their "love" is always going to be. Such people—and tragically, they seem to be the majority—are entirely unprepared for the rigors of mature love. A great number of them will soon become frustrated with their marriages and rush back out into the marketplace again to search for those lost fantasies.

Much of the reason for struggles of this kind lies in unwitting rejection of the deepest meaning of sexuality, for our sexuality calls us to far more than the physical enjoyment of our bodies. It calls us to enter into the inner parts of each other's souls, and there to know, honor, encourage, challenge, and comfort each other. Our sexuality demands that we love with integrity. We must be willing to call for the very best from our loved one, and we must be willing to accept that very same call from our beloved.

In the search for sexual fulfillment we should learn to be "lovers" in this matter of mutually challenging and correcting each other's lives. Unless we are willing to love in this way, no physical sexual relationship will be able to produce the fulfillment we seek. Single people will be very wise to change the focus from genital sex to mutual sharing with integrity.

Love Requires Humility

Hard love, however, requires that integrity be balanced by humility. To give myself to another in marriage (or any form of love relationship) requires that I hold on to my own integrity and self-respect and that I hold on to respect for the one I love. If I love, I will not behave as if I am the superior of the person I love. If love requires me to correct the one I love, I may do so only in humility, recognizing that I, too, may need to be corrected by the other in the next moment.

We all need to grow and mature in certain ways, no matter where we are in life. There is a lot of weakness, a lot of "rough edge," in each of us. In a sense we are still children who need guidance and discipline. We all need to be loved "toughly" (to use Dr. Dobson's term). But we will accept tough or judicious love only from those who we know accept us as we are, respect us as persons, and grant us forgiving grace.

The quality of humility causes us to remember how hard it is to be a child. Humility enables us to walk a mile in the other person's shoes, to feel his pain, to share his struggle. And humility helps us remember that we, too, are weak, frail, and inconsistent. Humility creates in us the gentleness and patience we need if we are to succeed at loving.

Vernon and Gladys were just about the sweetest Christian couple I ever met. They were married for sixty-three years before he died. Every time I was around them I could see the deep honor and confidence they had for each other. But the outstanding quality of their relationship was the obvious humility they felt toward each other. Whenever they spoke of each other it was plain to see that they had learned to adjust to each other's needs and desires many years before. There didn't seem to be any areas of conflict in their relationship. They seemed to move in tandem, understanding each other's needs, anticipating each other's concerns without needing to speak. They were wonderful to watch.

Once I asked them to explain their obvious respect and admiration for each other. Had it always been easy for them? Had they ever had conflict? Were they just naturally sweet people?

"Oh my, no," said Vernon. "We had a few whing-dings when we first got married, didn't we dear?" he said, smiling at Gladys.

Gladys just smiled and let him go on.

"But we made a decision early in our marriage that has always enabled us to deal with our differences in a loving and peaceful way," he said.

"And what was that?" I asked.

"We decided that we would always end the day with the question, 'Are we all right tonight?' Then if either one of us had a complaint of any kind, we would talk about it and pray about it before we went to sleep."

"And did it always work?" I wondered.

"Not always," Vernon replied. "I could be a stubborn old coot sometimes."

"Oh, Vernon, you weren't that stubborn," Gladys interrupted.

"Yes, I was too," he said. "You were just too kind to admit it."

"No, I wasn't always kind," she said.

"Yes, you were," Vernon said.

I shook my head in wonder at the two of them. Here they were in their mid-eighties arguing about who was the nicer of the two. Their humility before each other made them beautiful to behold.

To summarize, then, agape-love is the free giving of oneself in unconditional commitment to the growth and well-being of another person. Agape does not originate in one's own need or emotional attraction to the other person. Agape does not seek to possess or control the other person. Agape affirms the worth of the person loved—whatever the cost. Therefore, agape is forgiving and lasts *forever*.

But agape-love is not weak or passive. Agape is strong and reaches out actively for the growth and health of the person loved. Agape gives itself fully, but always judiciously, always with a view to what is best for the person loved. Agape is willing to fight hard for the good of the person loved. But agape is never proud or rough. Agape is humble, gentle, and respectful, for agape never forgets the value of the one loved.

This is the way I want to be loved. I want you to love me not because I am in some way attractive to you or useful to you. I want you to love me because you see some value in me entirely apart from my usefulness to you. Nor do I want your love for me to be conditioned upon some performance that I can give for your pleasure. I want you to love me because I need to be loved in those times when I cannot perform. I do not want your love at all if your love always demands that I please you.

But neither do I want you to pamper me. I want you to care enough about me that you will speak to me with honesty and integrity. I do not want you to criticize me or judge me, but I want your opposition when you think I am wrong. I want you to fight for me when I am about to throw myself away. I want your light when I am ready to plunge headlong into the darkness.

This is also the way in which I want to learn to love. I want to learn more about this kind of love as long as I live. I do not want to value others only for what they can do for me or only as long as they please me. I want my life to reach out to others without a price tag attached. I want a few people to know that I will always be there for them, no matter what it costs me. I want those I love to know that when I see their failures, I will face them with integrity. But I want them also to know, always to know, that I will never let them go. I can think of no higher achievement in life than to learn how to love with agape.

1. Morris, *Testaments of Love,* p. 128.
2. John Powell, *The Secret of Staying in Love* (Valencia, California: Tabor Publishing, 1974), pp. 46–57.
3. Ibid., p. 52.
4. Ibid.
5. Peck, *The Road Less Traveled,* p. 81.
6. Powell, *The Secret of Staying in Love,* p. 53.
7. Ibid., p. 54.
8. James Dobson, *Love Must Be Tough* (Waco, Texas: Word Inc., 1983).
9. Peck, *The Road Less Traveled,* p. 111.

CHAPTER 10

Sexual Growth and Fulfillment

W hy do I always strike out with women? No matter what I do, it just always seems to end up like this."

Hal stared at the floor and heaved a great exasperated sigh. He had been in my office before, usually with the same story and the same frustration. He had read a lot of those books about sexual fulfillment and fancied himself to be a "good lover." But his relationships with women were consistently shallow and brief.

"Hal, we've talked about all this before, and I still think you're failing to learn the real key to sexual fulfillment."

"Which is . . ."

"Which is that a relationship of real love is not the same thing as sexual desire."

"I understand that," Hal protested. "Jeanne was great sexually but she sure didn't love me."

Wondering if he realized what he had just said, I asked, "And just how important is that to you?"

"It's very important," he replied, "I really want to be loved. After all, having love is more important than having sex. Isn't that what you're always telling me?"

"Yes, it is," I answered. "But you seem to consistently rush your relationships with women into sexual activity before you develop genuine love. It's like you think that sexual closeness is going to automatically create a relationship of love. That's never going to work, and you ought to be seeing that by now."

"So tell me again, how do I do it right?"

Hal's struggle is the struggle of millions of modern people who believe that sex is the shortcut to love. But sexual activity by itself is like a house built on sand. It has no foundation. It cannot produce fulfillment.

The key to healthy sexual growth and fulfillment is in learning to develop relationships of agape-love. The Creator of our sexuality has given us this pattern. He who made our bodies and our spirits calls upon us to guide the passions of our bodies by the agape-love of our spirits.

I must never enter into a relationship with a person of the opposite sex with only physical sex *(eros)* on my mind. I must remember at the very beginning and throughout any relationship that the law of God requires me to subject my sexual urges and interests to the guidance of agape-love.

It is a very easy thing to begin to play at sex and forget to love. The excitement of a new involvement with an attractive person is heady stuff. It is the stuff the romantic fallacy thrives on. Foolish hearts sometimes rush into deep emotional attachments and even physical sexual arrangements without any consideration of whether agape-love is present.

But physical sexual activity without the spiritual strength of agape-love is wild and unruly business. It is the stuff broken hearts and disillusioned lives are made of. It may feel like a lot of fun for a while, but sooner or later our hearts will begin to ask us to answer the deeper, more spiritual questions of our sexual natures.

What is the meaning of our relationship? Where are we headed with each other? What is our purpose in being together? Such questions are only asking, Do we really love each other, or is this just the physical pleasure of sex? Do we intend to commit our lives to each other in the promises of agape-love, or is this just a trade of physical pleasures? Christian moral responsibility insists that we consider these questions first, before we plunge mindlessly into physical sexual activity. By answering them, we will be able to determine the emotional and physical expressions appropriate to our relationships.

Because our sexuality is far more than our capacity to do exciting things with our bodies, because it includes our ability (and our need) to enter into the lives of others in spiritual ways, agape-love is the secret of sexual fulfillment. Even married persons fail to achieve sexual fulfillment when they are attempting to find it only in physical sexual activity. Our sexuality cries out for spiritual intimacy with another, and physical sex alone cannot create such intimacy. Therefore, God requires us to know that we have agape-love before we enjoy the physical pleasures of our sexuality so that we will find the fulfillment we seek.

Here, then, is what I meant earlier when I suggested that it is possible for the single person to find genuine sexual fulfillment without the privilege of physical sex. Ultimately, sexual fullness and wholeness can be achieved only by those who look for it in the sharing of souls and work hard at learning the skills of such sharing. Of course, single people can learn to do this just as well as married people.

Generally speaking, the Bible says little about how we are to achieve sexual fulfillment. At least, the Scriptures do not use such terms. Yet clear scriptural principles provide guidance and direction regarding both sexual attitudes and behavior. As we learn to understand and apply those principles, we will grow as sexually fulfilled persons.

The Lord of Sexuality

The first principle of sexual fulfillment is the recognition of the Lord. Our sexuality is His creation, and He is properly the Lord over all that He has made. As His creatures, we have the duty to present to Him all and everything that we are, which includes our sexual natures.

The apostle Paul, in writing to the Roman church, spoke of the need to present ourselves totally to God:

> I beseech you therefore, brethren, by the mercies of God, that you present your bodies a living sacrifice, holy, acceptable to God which is your reasonable service. And do not be conformed to this world, but be transformed by the renewing of your mind, that you may prove what is that good and acceptable and perfect will of God (Rom. 12:1-2).

Paul's reasoning is powerful and inevitable for Christian singles. Since God, in His great mercy, has given us His Son and has cleansed us from our sins, we are called upon to live for Him. Because we are what we do with our bodies, our bodies must be wholly given—sacrificed—to the Lord! Instead of being governed and molded by the worldly society around us, we are to demonstrate in our daily conduct the good, acceptable, and perfect will of God.

To submit our sexuality to the Lord means two things. First, we must learn to say an emphatic "No!" to things God has forbidden. Our bodies were created to be used for the Lord, not for sexual immorality (1 Cor. 6:13), and that means genital sex is out for Christian singles. Sexual intercourse is the divine symbol of married love, and unmarried persons who love God will want to honor the heavenly Father by reserving intercourse for marriage.

For many people in our modern, "liberated" society, the idea of not doing something just because God said so seems outdated and useless as a moral principle. But I think that such people have no true love relationship with God. Persons who truly know our Father in heaven love Him deeply because He has given them so much. For those people, the commandments of God are not burdensome (1 John 5:3).

A good friend of mine tells the story of being taunted by his school chums because he did not want to participate with them in some illegal shenanigans. One of the boys asked, "What's the matter? Are you afraid your father will hurt you?" My friend responded, "No, I'm afraid that I will hurt my father."

My friend's love and respect for his father gave him strength and direction at a time when he greatly needed them. On a much higher level, Christian singles can see that sexual immorality would injure the heavenly Father. It is not fear of punishment but devotion and love that make them desire to remain pure.

A Positive Affirmation of Sexuality

Submitting sexuality to God's lordship is not only a matter of forgoing what God has forbidden. It is also a matter of saying a resounding "Yes!" to sexuality. Singles are never asked to deny their sexual natures; rather, they are to strongly affirm their sexuality in the ways that please God. This is the second broad principle of sexual fulfillment.

The will and the power of God have caused us to be sexual in nature. We are male and female with all that implies because God wished it to be so. Therefore, God calls upon us to be what we are as sexual creatures in a way that brings Him praise and produces wholeness for us. The prohibitions against sexual immorality in the Scriptures in no way indicate that God's attitude toward our sexuality is negative or that our attitudes should be negative.

Sexual fulfillment requires that we learn to affirm ourselves as sexual beings, whether we are married or unmarried. We are created with the God-given ability to give ourselves to others and to receive others into ourselves. In both body and soul we possess the potential to find fullness and wholeness in deep relatedness with others. This is God's wonderful gift to us, and we must affirm and celebrate it.

In seeking to affirm and celebrate our sexuality as single persons, we must not allow ourselves to be tripped up by unnecessary guilt or fear in regard to our sexuality. The sexual mistakes of the past may easily burden us with unresolved anxiety or guilt. We may have been deeply scarred by someone, or we may have injured others. The daily struggle with sexual tensions may frustrate and weary us to the point that we lose all hope of gaining control or making peace with our sexuality. Still, our sexuality is God's good gift to us, and if we will take the time to learn how to understand and use it, it can lead us to greater wholeness.

Serious Christians who have strong sex drives may experience difficulty finding the right balance between self-control and the positive affirmation of their sexuality. Once, while I was speaking on sexuality at a retreat, a woman asked me an intriguing question: "Did you ever just pray that God would take away your desire?"

"No," I replied, "but I often prayed for self-control. I think I always wanted to be a sexual being. I knew I was a man, and I was capable of developing a healthy sexual relationship with a woman if the time and circumstances were right. I never wanted to lose the desire."

"But sometimes for me," she went on, "my desires just seem to drive me crazy. I want so much to be with someone, and to feel loved. . . . It's just like a curse."

I certainly understood her feelings. And though the struggle with sexual tension may sometimes feel like a curse, it's not—it's a blessing. This woman's desire for sexual intimacy and the sense of being loved by someone is a wonderful part of her potential as God's creature to find wholeness in life. She is capable of finding completion in giving herself to a man. She ought to rejoice before God that she is woman, and that she possesses such potential. She also needs to know that it is possible to achieve much of her sexual potential through developing healthy sharing relationships without yielding to her desires for genital sex.

The Goal of Self-Sharing

Our sexuality demands far more than the sharing of our bodies. Sexuality is about the sharing of selves, our real, inmost, personal selves. This is the third principle for the development of sexual fulfillment and personal wholeness. Individuals who do not learn how to share themselves with others are doomed to lives of isolation, loneliness, and sexual frustration. No amount of genital sexual activity can fill the void created by the inability of people to share themselves.

Single Christians should set the goal of self-sharing for life. Instead of searching for opportunities to have genital sex, they should look for opportunities to develop intimacy on a truly personal level. There can never be any true sexual fulfillment without the experience of personal intimacy, but personal intimacy does not necessarily imply a genital relationship.

Richard J. Foster, in *Money, Sex and Power,* remarks,

> The single person's sexuality is expressed in his or her capacity to love and to be loved. Not all experiences of intimacy should eventuate in marriage or in genital sex. Loving does not need to be genital to be intimate, and the capacity to love is vital to our sexuality. And so the single person should develop many relationships that are wholesome and caring. Deeply affectionate but nongenital relationships are completely possible and should be encouraged.[1]

At this point many people will discover one of the most treacherous sexual pitfalls. How is it possible to develop personal intimacy without physical sexual involvement? It is a good question, and there are very good answers.

Intimacy and Sexuality

For many people, the very word *intimacy* implies physical sexual touching, but that is an unnecessary implication. Intimacy simply means drawing close to someone and being comfortable in that closeness. There are many ways of being close that do not involve sexual touching. I am being intimate any time that I reveal my true self to you and trust you with that knowledge.

The very best road to intimacy is talk. A good friend of mine says that *talk* is his favorite four-letter word. If we want to develop as self-sharing persons, we have to learn how to talk about our true selves. To do that, we have to discover the truth about ourselves and find the courage to disclose that truth to others.

A necessary corollary to this kind of self-revealing talk is the ability to trust. The lack of trust causes us to be cautious and self-guarding. It is natural to fear that if we honestly reveal the truth about ourselves, we might be rejected. But the other side of this matter is that unless we reveal the truth about ourselves, no one will be able to know who we really are, and no one will be able to love us. Our defenses and our masks keep us shielded from the love of other people. If we reveal only false selves to others, we can never be truly loved, for no one will know who we are.

The step of trust may be very difficult if I have been injured in a love relationship, but it is an absolute necessity for me to move toward wholeness as a person. Trust is the only pathway of escape from loneliness. If I do not trust anyone and, therefore, do not reveal my true self to anyone, no one will be my true friend. I may have many superficial relationships, but I will have no honest ones.

Loneliness is one of the greatest causes of sexual distress and sorrow. Loneliness, far more than mere physical desire, drives strangers into bed with each other. Here again, we can see the spiritual side of sexuality coming into the picture. As sexual beings, humans have natural longings to find fulfillment in sharing themselves with another person. But because most people have learned so little about self-sharing, they are easily tempted to move quickly past the spiritual dimension and physically share bodies.

A word of caution is necessary. Recently single-again people may experience almost unbearable loneliness, and they may misinterpret their longing for intimacy with another to be a merely physical sexual need.

I remember having a conversation that demonstrates what I am talking about. The fellow had been married for over twenty years and had been generally happy with the marriage. As he described his sexual relationship with his wife, he indicated that they continued to have a sexual relationship right up to the end of their time of living together. When I asked him, he told me that they had been accustomed to having intercourse about once a week or every ten days. He was quite happy with that frequency.

But when his wife left him, he was driven by urgent physical sexual desires. He began to masturbate for the first time in many years. And he would masturbate every day, sometimes more than once. What was wrong with him? That was his question for me. Why, after being rather calm in matters of physical sex for years, was he so needy?

I think the answer is partly, if not largely, in his great loneliness. He was a Christian man who did not believe he ought to rush out to find another woman. In fact, he wanted to remain faithful to his wife in the hope that she might return to him. Therefore, he had no avenues of sexual expression open to him.

When his wife was with him, there were many forms of sexual expression between them. They had intercourse once every ten days, perhaps, but they expressed themselves in many other truly sexual ways. They could talk and touch and hold each other and, at the very least, land in bed side by side at the end of a weary day. All of these were legitimate ways of expressing their intimacy, and each one added a certain sense of belonging to his life. Now he had no one to talk with, no one to touch caringly, and no one in the bed beside him at night. The loneliness was deep, and it is no coincidence that he soon felt strong genital urges.

This man's experience represents that of numerous people, both men and women, who have spoken to me at Fresh Start Seminars about their first weeks and months after they were left alone. For many, the consequences were more tragic because they wound up in sexual rebound relationships and eventually were scarred even more deeply. The final results of the relationships were often a more profound sense of distrust and an unwillingness to share, which led to a more intense loneliness.

These people needed an opportunity to share themselves honestly and openly in a sexually safe environment. I suggested to my friend that he become involved in a church-related support group that I knew about. Within a couple of months he told me that he had begun to develop some very good friendships with both men and women. He felt that some people understood him and cared about him. He was starting to feel that he truly belonged to someone again. What's more, he was no longer so driven by sexual desire. He had not quit masturbating, but his need for it was markedly reduced. As his loneliness had eased, so had the intensity of his sexual urges.

Because there are so many sexual pitfalls for single-again persons, I would strongly recommend that they go very slowly and cautiously in developing new intimate relationships. At first, it is best to seek same-sex friends. Later, I would encourage associating with groups of strong and responsible Christian singles who can be a source of encouragement, understanding, and support. Such groups can provide a healthy source of emotional fulfillment through warm, personal relationships.

Gradually, persons who are learning to share in same-sex relationships and in healthy group relationships will develop the strength to reveal their true selves to members of the opposite sex without great vulnerability to physical sexual temptation. Gaining true intimacy with others will reduce the urgency of physical desires.

"How in the world can you grow intimate with someone and not be turned on by physical sexual desires?" she asked. Yvonne had been seeing me for several months to discuss her problem. Often we talked about her recurring sexual struggles with men. She was learning a lot, but my new teaching troubled her. For her, strong emotional feelings of intimacy had always led to genital expression. Separating the two things seemed impossible.

"I think there are two answers," I said. "First, as you truly share yourself with another person and allow that person to share with you, you will grow to see each other in much broader perspectives than merely as potential sex partners."

"You mean, not just as sex objects," she said.

"Right. You will learn to value each other for different reasons. And that will mean you will begin to find some real sense of satisfaction and fulfillment in nurturing and strengthening each other in those parts of your lives."

"Oh, I understand that, I think," she replied. "I mean, I certainly understand it with women. I've had some really good relationships with women friends in which we got very close to each other."

"And your relationship was not in any way sexually oriented?"

"Of course not!" she snapped. "If there's anything you should be sure of by now, it's my heterosexuality."

"Oh, I'm sure of that," I said, "but my point is that intimacy is not the same thing as physical or genital expression."

"Sure," she said, "but how does this apply to relationships with men?"

"The lesson is quite simple, really," I replied. "There are many ways to be intimate with someone that have nothing to do with physical sexual expression, whether that person is a man or a woman."

"I can understand that," she said, "but when the other person is a man, I can never get the sexual thing off my mind."

"Well, suppose the man were your father or your brother? Would you have a sexual problem then?" I asked.

"That's different," she answered, "and you know it."

"But why is it different?" I asked her. "There have been relatives who have been sexually involved."

"Yeah, but not me. I could never do that. It just wouldn't be right."

I pressed the point. "But why wouldn't it be right? Why couldn't you go to bed with your brother?"

"Because it just isn't that kind of a relationship," she almost shouted at me.

"But if the two of you wanted to have that kind of relationship, you could choose to do it."

She looked puzzled by my direction. "So what are you trying to get at?" she asked.

"I'm getting at the second answer to your question about how to have a truly intimate relationship without its becoming sexually expressive."

"Which is?"

"Which is that you have to make choices about your behavior."

"You're saying I can just choose to have a relationship with a man that is not sexually oriented if I decide to," she said.

"That's right," I replied. "You can choose to grow close to a man in ways that will allow you to be his good friend without choosing to express friendship in ways centered on your genital urges."

"But what would be the point?"

I wish I could tell you that Yvonne finally got the point, but as far as I know, she never did. The point is that we do, in fact, choose the nature and the parameters of our relationships. We choose how we will think of others and how we will think of ourselves in relationship with them. And we choose how we will behave toward them.

Christian singles must choose behavior consistent with the revealed will of God. We have been called to develop intimate relationships with others, which includes our Christian brothers and sisters. But because we have also been called to avoid sexual immorality, we must exercise our wills in accordance with God's will. We can choose both true intimacy and sexual purity.

In his book *Being Sexual . . . and Celibate,* Keith Clark, a Capuchin monk, relates the story of his relationship with a dear female friend named Jan. For ten years they had known each other and were quite fond of each other. He grew to have very strong romantic feelings for her, but never chose to act upon them because of his vows of celibacy. Eventually, he told her of the nature of his feelings for her. I will let him tell the rest:

> That was the first time I told her directly of my romantic inclinations toward her. And that was the first time that she told me that she had felt the same way toward me all along!
>
> The romantic feelings we had each harboured for almost 10 years were now spoken. She told me she simply had come to love and respect me too much to do or say anything which would have taken me away from my commitment to religious life. I loved and respected her too much to

try to involve her in a romantic relationship which couldn't go anywhere without upsetting a lot of lives. During those years, there was no need to speak our feelings directly, because there had been no indirect mixed messages in our behaviour which needed explaining. When we did tell each other about our feelings it had quite a different meaning, I suspect, than it would have had we spoken our feelings at the beginning when we could have allowed them to overpower us. Ten years later our speaking could be a statement disclosing our feelings; the behaviour we had chosen toward each other those 10 years precluded any mixed messages in our disclosure now.

These past years have seen our love deepen. I knew from the outset that if I would have left my religious commitment and pursued the possibility of marrying Jan, our romantic feelings would find expression in the concrete actions of establishing and maintaining a family. I knew a commitment to Jan in marriage would mature our romantic inclinations for each other into *intimacy* that would find expression in romantic and genital ways. What I didn't know was that love can mature whether or not two people marry.[2]

This situation illustrates the kind of decision making that needs to occur if we are to learn how to establish intimate relationships without violating God's rules for sexual expression. Clark describes some other intimate relationships and then summarizes how behavioral choices have helped them in the development of intimacy:

Intimacy could grow *because of the way we behaved toward each other*. The behaviours I chose allowed a personal intimacy to grow instead of merely relationships which would be gratifying to my genital urges and romantic drives or would simply find me filling a role which related to the role which another filled. . . .

. . . That's the way it is with personal relationships, I believe. We are motivated to enter them because of functional necessity, genital urges, emotional and romantic drives and a personal need for intimacy. What motivates us is not that which shaped the relationship; the behaviour we choose is what allows relationships to develop into personally intimate ones.[3]

Most of the Christian singles I meet have not taken religious vows of celibacy. But Clark's story has valuable lessons for all of us. It is possible to choose to draw close to people, even those of the opposite sex, and to develop truly intimate relationships without violating God's standards for the unmarried. Furthermore, there are ways in which genital activity, if it is the primary force in a relationship, can actually block the development of true intimacy.

Jerry and Barbara were a married couple who discovered that their relationship was becoming dull and listless. When they went to the counselor they were confused. Their sexual relationship was satisfactory, they said. They had intercourse about once a week, and they were both content with that. But Barbara reported that she often felt unloved after they had had intercourse, and Jerry was detecting her feelings of disappointment with him.

"What else are you doing to help create intimacy?" the counselor asked.

"What do you mean?" Jerry asked.

"What do you do, on a regular basis, besides intercourse, to draw close to each other?" the counselor replied.

Jerry and Barbara looked puzzled for a moment. Then Barbara said, "Not much really. We almost never talk."

"We talk," Jerry contradicted.

Suddenly Barbara was angry. "When, Jerry?" she snapped. "When do we talk? I mean personally, about us, about what's inside?"

Jerry was silent.

The simple formula the counselor then recommended worked wonders for their relationship. He suggested that they have intercourse no more than once a month for three months. But he also suggested that they plan to have at least one hour alone together two nights a week during those three months. During that special hour there could be no distractions. No TV, no reading material, the phone off the hook. They could touch, but they could not hold each other closely or become involved in kissing or fondling.

They were to spend the hour talking about themselves. They were to share their feelings about each other and about anything else that seemed important to share. If strong disagreement arose during their discussions they were to write those things down as subjects to discuss with the counselor, and, for the time, they were to avoid any further discussion of the problem area. After three months, they reported a deepening of their relationship and an increased sense of trust and respect. Their sense of intimacy was much stronger even though they had had intercourse much less frequently.

"It was as if we had forgotten how to be personal with each other,"

Barbara said. "We had made sex the focus of our times together, and we were losing ourselves in the process."

By developing the skills of sharing ourselves with others and committing ourselves to godly behavior patterns toward others, we can create the foundations of personal intimacy and fulfillment. Unless these become our goals, we are inevitably going to fail in our search for sexual fulfillment. Genital sexual activity alone cannot deliver what our souls seek.

The Development of Self-Control

The fourth principle of sexual fulfillment is that single persons who choose to observe God's rules for single life have to learn to control their sexual behavior, which, of course, is a great source of conflict. Individuals who seek counseling in this area rarely ask whether they ought to control themselves. They ask instead *how* to control themselves.

The normal needs for intimacy and sexual fulfillment are strong, and the world sends powerful messages that argue against restraint and make us feel that we are strange if we want to control ourselves. How can we learn self-control?

Perhaps we would do well to begin by speaking of a major false assumption of our modern society—that genital sexual activity is a basic life need. Popular entertainment personalities and numerous professional people daily shout the message that if you are not sexually active, you probably have something wrong with you. Sex is normal and natural, they say, and the plainly taught implication is that sexual activity is not only permissible but necessary for healthy life. In the end, sexual intercourse is advocated as a life necessity.

This assertion is simply false. There are some basic life needs, but sexual intercourse is not one of them. To live, we need to eat and drink and breathe. If we don't, we will die. Sexual intercourse, in its proper place, can be a nurturing and enriching part of life, but if you go without it, you will not die. I promise that you will never read the headline in the morning news: MAN DIES—NO SEX!

If we are going to successfully control ourselves in this matter of our sexuality, we need to tell ourselves the truth. The truth is that many people have lived quite full, productive, and happy lives without being active in genital sexuality. And that does not mean they have been sexually miserable and unfulfilled people.

Martha Smith Good writes,

There is a distinction between "affective" sexuality, and "genital" sexuality. Affective sexuality embodies the spiritual, emotional, and psychological aspects of our humanness. Affective sexuality reaches out to include the whole area of emotional warmth given only to those created in the image of God. In essence, it is the totality of all that we are as we express ourselves, individually and corporately, in our relatedness as male and female in friendship and in fellowship. . . .

. . . the single individual who has had the opportunity to face the reality of discovering affective sexuality experientially may be as sexually mature, if not more so, than the person in a marriage relationship where sexuality as genital sex is taken for granted. Single persons who can freely and comfortably respond to both males and females with love, gentleness, and compassion are most likely in touch with their affective sexuality. This in no way implies an absence of genital feelings. It does suggest, though, that these persons have acquired a broad understanding of sexuality and recognize that genital sex is not the only means of sexual expression.[4]

I am convinced that Mrs. Good is right. In my experience of living alone for fourteen years after a divorce I learned that men and women can relate to each other with compassion and caring and can physically touch in affirming and comforting ways that do not lead to genital sexual expression. In recent years, I have met many strong Christian singles who have triumphantly traveled much the same path. They are not active in genital sex, but they are some of the most sexually mature and fulfilled people I know.

The first step in learning to control ourselves sexually, then, is simply to recognize that it is quite possible to do so and quite healthy as well. God is not victimizing us by commanding that we reserve full sexual expression for marriage. Certainly, it can be difficult, even painful for a time, for those who are single again to adjust to the celibate life. But celibacy is not death, and neither is it sickness.

The second thing we need to realize about self-control is that it is an indication of strength. All strong people have mastered the disciplines of self-control. There are few qualities that we admire more than self-control. In any field of endeavor those who have earned our respect and applause are people of great self-mastery. Athletes, musicians, scientists, military men, and countless others have achieved their successes by gaining control over their weaknesses and errors. To gain self-control in sexual awareness and behavior ought also to be something we applaud in others and desire for ourselves.

Here are some suggestions for persons struggling with sexual self-control.

Make a Commitment

Self-control is impossible for persons who will not make a commitment to it. Self-control begins with a hard and clear decision to be a certain kind of person. Single persons who toy around with their commitment only guarantee their failure at self-control. But persons who honestly determine to refrain from sexual intercourse outside marriage can succeed.

I want to emphasize the certainty of success for those who make a personal commitment to avoid sexual behavior that violates God's rules. I am not talking about careless or halfhearted words of commitment. I am talking about *real* determination.

On many occasions I have heard individuals state that they do not have the power to control themselves in sexual matters. They seem to believe that once their glands begin to do their thing that full sexual expression is automatic and inevitable. But no one is ever under the control of his glands. Glands do not have the power to make decisions. We are always capable of controlling ourselves if we make serious commitment to self-control.

I have often used this illustration to make the point that we can control ourselves far better than we sometimes think. Imagine yourself in a completely vulnerable sexual situation. You and some wonderful lover are all heated up and at the very threshold of sexual intercourse. Nothing can stop you now, right? Then your partner says, "I'm not sure if I've told you or not, but I have AIDS." Question—can you control yourself?

People usually chuckle a little and agree that when it is a matter of life and death even the powerful genital urge can be controlled. My point is that our modern attitude of weakness is not based on the fact that sexual desires are just too strong to resist but on the fact that in our prevailing moral climate many simply do not perceive that there is any reason to control themselves. A person who sincerely believes that God's rules point him in the direction of maximum fulfillment, and who truly wants to commit himself to a life of sexual morality, will be able to keep his commitment.

Be Honest with Oneself

An essential ingredient in self-control is honesty with oneself. Persons who have made a commitment to stay out of compromised sexual situations, for example, will not lie to themselves about their motives in personal relationships. Nor will they lie to themselves about their relative strengths and weaknesses. They will be honest! They will admit to themselves when they are tempted to do what is contrary to their commitment, and they will admit that they are weak enough to yield to the temptation. One wonders how many sexual tragedies might have been avoided if people had known how to be honest with themselves.

A young man named Ross was very active in a youth program I worked with years ago. We had talked about sexual standards many times. He said he wanted to remain sexually pure until marriage, but he felt weak and worried that one day he would fall. One day he came to see me with the sad report.

"Well, I did it," he said disgustedly.

"Did what?" I asked.

"You know what I'm talking about. I did what I knew I would do."

"Are you telling me that you and Laura have had intercourse?"

"Yes."

"What happened?" I asked.

"What do you mean?" he pleaded. "I don't know; it just happened."

"It just happened?" I blurted in amazement. "It just happened? You two were just walking down the street the other night, minding your business, and suddenly, without warning, BAM, it just happened?"

"No, of course not, it wasn't that way. You know how it happened."

"Sure do," I said.

After that we walked through the painful reality of what had happened to Ross and Laura. What had happened, of course, was that they had made a series of decisions. First, they had gone to a very private place, then they had begun to pet, then they had begun to open each other's clothes, and, finally, they had removed their clothes and chosen together to have intercourse. It did not just happen. It happened because they chose to make it happen. Either one of them could have interrupted the process at any point by saying honestly that he or she did not want to go further.

This matter of honesty is closely related to self-sharing and self-discovery. Many people cannot be honest with themselves because they do not know themselves very well. They are often frustrated with themselves as they discover their inability to do what they say they will do. They make certain promises—and they feel strongly when they make them—but then they fail to keep their word. The problem often is that they just are not in touch with certain real parts of their personalities.

Seek the Support of Others

By sharing ourselves with others, talking about what we feel and think on an intimate level, we often discover things about ourselves that we never knew before. Through that process, we uncover fears and anxieties and motivations within our hearts that we do not understand. And in coming to terms with these inmost discoveries about ourselves, we can develop the ability to make strong decisions about our lives.

Another way in which it can be helpful to share ourselves openly and honestly with others is that we can gain a sense of shared strength and accountability. When others know of our inmost struggle and encourage and strengthen us, we will have a sense of greater strength when we are alone. We will also have a sense of accountability.

Probably nothing ever gave me greater personal strength in my own struggle to regain a sexual balance than when a good friend promised me that he was going to ask me direct questions about my thought life and conduct every time we got together. Since we were getting together weekly, that added strength of self-control to my inner resolve to grow and be strong. I knew I would have to face him, and that helped me face myself. Good friends should do such things for each other.

Avoid Tempting Situations

Persons who honestly seek to avoid sinful behavior will also avoid situations that offer temptations to sinful behavior. Numerous examples are obvious. Certain types of music are powerful sexual stimulants. The same is true of TV programming, movies, magazines, and books. Persons who desire self-control need to know what things are most likely to tempt them and stay away from them!

It is also advisable to stay out of social gatherings designed to be sexually supercharged. Singles bars, night clubs with sexually explicit entertainment, and the like are not very good places to learn self-control.

Another obviously tempting situation to avoid is privacy with persons of the opposite sex. At the Fresh Start Seminars I always recommend that single-again people refrain from dating for about two years. Of course, that figure is arbitrary, but persons need some strength of self-control before dating. In our society it is nearly impossible to date without romantic overtones and times of privacy. Even strong people need to be cautious and watch their step in this matter of privacy. I doubt if any of my readers need proof of what I am saying. There really is no substitute for good sense, you know.

Develop Spiritual Discipline

More important than anything in regard to inner strength and self-control is the development of spiritual discipline. By that I mean establishing regular, daily habits of worship through meditation on the Scriptures and prayer. Nothing strengthens the inner heart like drawing close to God in honesty.

Perhaps you have never done this kind of thing before and feel the need for help. Many people are available to guide you in these efforts, such as a pastor or some other Christian worker. If you have attended a Fresh Start program, perhaps you could find someone involved in leadership at the sponsoring church to work with you.

No matter what other helps and support systems we may have, we should present ourselves to God (Rom. 12:1) to ask for His Spirit's presence and power. Coming into God's presence with our weaknesses, our sins, and our confusion will provide direction, cleansing, and strength. Nothing can substitute for this!

One of my favorite Scripture passages is Ephesians 3:16–19. It has become familiar encouragement to me in my journey. I offer it as an encouragement to you:

> I pray that out of [God's] glorious riches he may strengthen you with power through his Spirit in your inner being, so that Christ may dwell in your hearts through faith. And I pray that you, being rooted and established in love, may have power, together with all the [people of God], to grasp how wide and long and high and deep is the love of Christ, and to know this love that surpasses knowledge—that you may be filled to the measure of all the fullness of God (NIV).

If you come to God Himself, He will give you His love, which will provide a new kind of inner fullness. That fullness is the very presence of His Spirit within your heart. Through His Spirit, you can grow strong in faith and personal discipline of your life.

However, you will not automatically become some superhuman being who never has a struggle. You will still be human, and you will still have to fight daily battles of self-discipline and self-control. But you will not be alone. God will give you His special strength, and you will sense that strength in different ways at different times.

Sometimes it will be simple awareness or alertness to spiritual values. Sometimes it will be an inner serenity just when you were starting to come apart. Often it will be the courage to resist a tempting situation. Mostly, it will be the quieting and healing assurance that God is with you, loving you, forgiving you, guiding you, and helping you to be what He has called you to be.

Leaving Marriage in God's Hands

In searching for sexual fulfillment, Christian singles must recognize a fifth principle—to place the question of marriage in the hands of God alone. Marriage is not part of His plan for everyone. Even though it may be painful to face, divorced persons must recognize that they may never marry again.

I want to emphasize this point because many single people make the mistake of thinking of marriage as an unqualified goal for their lives. People who do that will often have great difficulty learning what they need to learn about themselves as persons and, in particular, reaching a healthy understanding of their sexuality.

The person who makes marriage the only goal may easily short-circuit the lessons about self-sharing I described earlier. If marriage matters most, a person may move toward it rapidly without thinking about what other things in life need to be done.

Suppose, for example, that you get involved with someone romantically, and after six weeks, that person suggests marriage. If you have decided that marriage is your primary goal, you may agree without giving any serious consideration to whether or not it is a wise or an appropriate move for you. There are many good reasons why some people should not marry, and you may be ignoring some that apply to you.

Have you learned the lessons of self-sharing? Have you learned how to reveal yourself honestly and how to trust others with the knowledge of who you truly are? Does your new love interest really know you well enough to make a whole-life commitment to you? Are there children involved? How will they feel? How will their presence in the home affect the proposed marriage? These are questions many people simply will not ask themselves if they are committed to marriage as an unqualified personal goal.

Unexamined motives often drive people toward marriage. One person may desire marriage just to solve the problem of loneliness. Another may marry to gain help in raising children. Some people get married to solve financial problems. And, of course, many marry only to satisfy the genital urge. These may be selfish and, therefore, entirely unacceptable reasons for getting married.

People should not even think about marriage if they do not believe they have grown to maturity as persons able to share themselves honestly, trust others, and make and keep promises. In the end the happiness and the wholeness of every marriage depend on the ability of the two people involved to keep the promise of lifelong commitment.

The rising divorce rate in our country is well known. What is not so well known is that the divorce rate for second marriages is even higher, and beyond that, the divorce rate for those who enter a second marriage within two years after a divorce is highest of all. Clearly, single-again persons are at high risk if they choose to marry again, especially if they act quickly. Marriage is no solution for personal weaknesses or problems. Persons who have gone through a divorce should know that.

Christian singles must not assume that marriage is necessarily in God's plans for their lives. They must accept the possibility that they will never marry and come to terms with the fact that a fulfilled and happy life is quite possible, even if they always remain single. Single persons need to focus not on getting married but on developing into individuals who share with others on a deep and personal level. They must emphasize learning the skills of agape-love in relationships. As they do so, they will develop the very aspects of their nature required to have a balanced and whole sexuality.

An interesting thing will happen to persons who come to terms with the possibility that they will never marry and also determine to grow as self-sharing persons. They will gradually learn that they do not have to get married to become happy and fulfilled. Instead of concentrating on the supposed need to be married, they will invest themselves in the lives of others and learn to share. They will also increase their self-mastery and self-control.

The result will be a strong, positive attitude toward their sexuality. They will view their sexuality as a gift from God that helps them grow as individuals. Finally, they will be able to submit their sexuality to the guidance of God as they grow and as they determine whether or not it is right to marry.

The relationship that God gave to Reidun and me during the ten years that we were "going together" was a wonderful affirmation of this truth. Very early in our relationship we talked about what the Lord requires of single persons. We knew that intercourse was always forbidden to the unmarried, and we pledged ourselves to honor the Lord and each other in the way we conducted ourselves together. Little did we know at that time what a lengthy relationship we were to have as single friends.

After we had known each other for about three years and had grown to care very deeply for each other, we had a kind of crisis experience. I knew by then that I wanted to marry Reidun and I told her so. She did not respond well to the idea. She told me that she did not think she would ever want to marry again. She also told me that if I wanted to look for someone else that she would understand it, and that she would set me free from our relationship with only good and positive memories of our times together.

At that time we were living over a hundred miles apart and did not see each other very frequently. It was nearly three weeks before I saw her again, but in the meantime I had made a very solid decision about how I would relate to her. I told her that I would rather continue to be her close friend and remain unmarried forever than ever be anyone else's husband.

Reidun questioned whether I really knew what I was saying, but there was no doubt in my mind. I knew that she meant what she had said and believed that we probably would never be married. I also knew that our commitment to the Lord would require us to accept a celibate life-style. It was my intention to love her as a single man and to accept God's rules of our conduct.

Through the next seven years of our relationship, the Lord enabled us to walk with Him and to honor His lordship over our sexuality. I will not claim that we were never tempted sexually, but God always gave us the strength and self-control we needed to keep our relationship clean before Him. We never had intercourse until we were married, and we have always considered that to be one of the best gifts that we have given to each other.

Something wonderful happened to us during those seven years. We grew to know each other in many other ways. We loved each other, and we were often affectionate. We shared life in many forms. We worked together (she has a large house, with a lot of grass to cut); we enjoyed our kids together (there are nine); and we talked about everything. Through those years we developed a great understanding of each other's needs and special struggles and a deep respect for each other as persons. Nothing could have been a better foundation for marriage.

At a seminar a woman once asked us, "How could you wait so long to get married?" The answer has two parts, I suppose. First of all, there were a number of very concrete obstacles to marriage that we needed to confront. I will not list them in detail, but I will tell you that one was our firm agreement that we should raise our children before we gave consideration to the possibility of marriage. We had strong convictions that a blended family would be unwise for us.

The second part of the answer is that those seven years never felt like we were waiting for anything. I imagine that the woman's question presumed that marriage was our true goal all along. Seven years would be a long time to wait if one were counting the days until he could be married. But marriage was not our goal. The relationship itself—knowing each other and loving each other as we were, being faithful in our relationship, and seeking to encourage each other in our service to the Lord we love— was the goal. We did not talk of marriage often or give it serious consideration until the last months before we actually married. When the moment did come and the decision to marry was made, it took only a few weeks to accomplish it. We were well prepared.

I certainly would not expect anyone to use our experience as a norm. No doubt, our story is a bit unusual. But I would plead with anyone who searches for sexual fulfillment to recognize that its true basis is the kind of relationship that Reidun and I were able to develop during our relationship before marriage. Because we were able to put sexual matters in perspective and focus on loving each other as whole persons, we were able to grow in personal awareness and appreciation of the manifold ways in which a man and woman can grow in love.

All of this may sound as if I am not in favor of marriage. Of course, I favor marriage when it is right for the two people involved. But I know from hard experience that marriage is often not right at all. Maturity and strength are essential to do well in marriage, especially if the two people have been previously injured in love.

Surely most of my readers know that marriage can be a very unsatisfying and even destructive state when either one or both partners are immature, weak, or relationally unskilled. Primarily because of the great potential for destructiveness, I say that marriage should never be an unqualified goal for anyone.

One final word needs to be given about sexual fulfillment. I have suggested that sexual fulfillment is a real possibility for single people who follow God's sexual rules. Obviously, single Christians will not be able to have everything that their sexuality desires or promises; they will not have the option of sexual intercourse.

But that will not keep them from sexual growing and fulfillment because they understand sexuality as a spiritual as well as a physical dimension of life. Within the boundaries of responsible self-sharing and self-control they will discover a tremendous potential for personal fulfillment and satisfaction as sexual beings.

What, then, are sexually fulfilled persons? The answer is basically the same for single and married persons. Sexually fulfilled persons affirm the basic God-given goodness of their sexuality and accept their responsibility for self-control in honoring the guidelines of God in their sexual choices. Their primary goals involve sharing their lives with others in relationships of agape-love, and not in genital activity.

For sexually fulfilled persons, genital sex properly belongs to marriage alone, and marriage is a possibility only if God clearly leads an individual and a potential life-mate to a whole-life commitment. They are fulfilled because they have learned what and who they are as sexual creatures of God and because they are growing into the whole persons they want to be.

1. Richard J. Foster, *Money, Sex and Power* (San Francisco: Harper & Row, 1985), p. 115.
2. Keith Clark, *Being Sexual . . . and Celibate* (Notre Dame: Ave Maria Press, 1986), p. 98.
3. Ibid., p. 102.
4. Martha Smith Good, in *Single Voices,* ed. Bruce and Imo Jeanne Yoder, (Scottdale, Pennsylvania: Herald Press, 1982), pp. 67–68.

CHAPTER 11

Single
Sexual
Relationships

Bruce and Karen are very special Christian people. As we walked along the beautiful trail through the woods on a bright day last fall, they revealed some of that specialness to me.

"We need your help in a very difficult and sensitive area," Bruce told me. He reached over to take Karen's hand and tenderly looked into her eyes. She looked at him, glanced quickly at me, and then looked at the ground. I was pretty sure I knew what was coming. I encouraged him to go on.

"Karen and I have been seeing each other for close to a year now," he continued, "and we love each other very much."

"I'm very happy to hear that," I said. I had known them both for some time and had genuine respect for them as Christian people who had suffered as the result of broken marriages. Individually, they had shared many of their trials with me. Their love for the Lord was very obvious to me. Until that day I had not known of their personal involvement, however.

Bruce did not seem to know how to proceed, so I asked, "Bruce, is this conversation going to be about sex?"

"Yes, . . . it is," he said. "We are just finding it hard to know . . . , well, to know what we should do."

"Do you mean you have questions about how you should behave with each other in expressing your love?" I asked.

"Yes," said Karen, "like Bruce said, we love each other very much, and we think we may get married someday, although right now that's really not possible. But . . . ," she hesitated.

"But sometimes it gets a little warm?" I asked.

"Yes," she said, looking directly at me, "we just aren't sure what we can and cannot do together. Don't misunderstand. We haven't slept together, and we won't. We know what God's standards are, and we want to honor Him in our relationship. But we need to know what is legitimate for us. I mean, how much can we love each other?"

"Do you mean how far can you go?" I asked.

"Right," Bruce chimed in, "it's just that it seems so right to touch Karen, but when it becomes more intimate, sometimes we wonder if we are being what God wants us to be. The Bible doesn't really say anything about petting, does it?"

How should unmarried persons conduct themselves? What forms of sexual expression, if any, are permissible between singles who love? It is true that the Bible does not speak directly to questions about the propriety of petting between single people. So, what shall we say to people like Bruce and Karen? Should we view all sexual touch prior to marriage as being sinful before God? Or are some forms of sexually intimate touch permitted between singles? If so, how are we to identify those forms of touch? Does the Bible provide any guidance in these areas?

The Confusion Among Christians

These are hard questions, and there are no simple answers. Because the Bible does not speak specifically on these issues, Christian authorities who venture to discuss them disagree widely about how to advise single people. Many will say that any and all sexually expressive touch between singles is sinful. These people consider all forms of sexual expression to be steps in an inevitable process leading to sexual intercourse. Since intercourse is forbidden to the unmarried, all of these "preliminary" steps are also forbidden.

Others believe that it is possible for unmarried people to express love and affection with physical touch in ways consistent with Christian moral principles. Their reasoning is that the purpose of physical affection is not necessarily to lead people to intercourse; it may legitimately express mutual caring and intimate sharing without having intercourse as the inevitable result.

Those who believe that all sexually expressive touch should be forbidden for singles will argue that once such behavior begins, there is no turning back the passions. Sooner or later, petting will inevitably lead to intercourse. To view it in any other way is, in their thinking, to rationalize for sinful behavior.

Those who are on the other side of the issue believe that it is a mistake to lump all types of sexual touch together as if they could lead only to one possible conclusion. To treat all extramarital sexual touch as if it were sinful is only to create false and unnecessary guilt in people and, possibly, to thwart the healthy growth of relationships.

While Christian scholars debate and hand down their opinions, Christian singles struggle for balanced understanding of the will of God. How shall we understand the Bible's teaching as it applies to our behavior in dating and courtship? Is it possible to find hard and sure answers for every situation? If not, what principles guide us through the gray areas?

What Is in the Heart?

Before we consider specific questions regarding how single people may touch each other, let's think about what goes on inside the heart. All questions about personal sexual behavior are first of all questions about the heart. And the heart can be a considerable problem. The Bible warns us that, ultimately, all evil begins in and proceeds from the heart. Jesus taught, "For out of the heart proceed evil thoughts, murders, adulteries, fornications. . . . These are the things which defile a man" (Matt. 15:19–20). More than that, the heart is not to be trusted. As Jeremiah declared, "The heart is deceitful above all things, and desperately wicked; who can know it?" (Jer. 17:9).

Speaking specifically of sexual sins of the heart, Jesus said, "Whoever looks at a woman to lust for her has already committed adultery with her in his heart" (Matt. 5:28). In His statement Jesus was arguing against the superficial righteousness of His day. People tended to measure themselves in terms of their actual deeds and ignored the inner state of their hearts before God. With this approach a man could tell himself that he was sexually pure so long as he had not actually done the deed of adultery.

Jesus was saying that adultery, like all sins, originates in the inner being. The lust of the heart of a man for a woman (or a woman for a man) is also sinful. It is possible to be guilty of vile sin in the heart without touching anyone. The point is that when God evaluates us, He searches the depths of our hearts.

Reasoning from Bible passages such as these, the church has always taught, and quite properly so, that the Christian must beware not only of evil deeds but also of evil thoughts and motives. Moral questions, therefore, concern actions, intentions, and desires. It is possible to do all the right things on the surface of life, but still be guilty of great evil because the heart is filled with lust or covetousness.

Christian singles will recognize that they must guard their hearts from lust. It is not enough to avoid sexual intercourse outside marriage. Nor is it enough to establish rules or parameters for affectionate touch between the sexes. Ultimately, Christian moral responsibility requires persons to deal with the lust of the heart. Powerful and deceptive forces within the heart must be faced honestly if individuals are to make truly moral decisions.

It is possible, however, to interpret these teachings about the lust of the heart too severely. The Church has often been careless and unbalanced in its instruction on this matter of the lust of the heart—at least that is how it seems to me. In many cases the church has at least implied that *all* sexual thoughts and feelings in the heart are necessarily evil and, therefore, ought to be repressed outside marriage. The tragic result of such teaching has been that generations of Christian single people have felt a greatly disproportionate sense of guilt about their sexual thought life, a terrible burden of self-condemnation, and a general sense of moral failure and disillusionment about living the Christian life.

I remember a personal experience that illustrates this point rather well. I was twenty years old, a college student, and a zealous, growing Christian. It was a warm spring night, and I was hard at work on some assignment in the college library. At some point I needed to walk through the stacks to find a book. There I encountered one of the college girls coming my way. She was quite attractive and I must admit that I had noticed her before, but I had never gotten that close to her. We passed each other in the narrow passage, and my arm brushed her arm.

A rush of feeling swept through me when we touched. I immediately felt an inner reaction of guilt and self-condemnation. I was at that time becoming very serious about the Christian life and was working hard on learning how to discipline my life. One of the areas of concern to me was maintaining a sexually pure heart. Having brushed that delightful girl's arm, I was feeling impure. I left the library and walked around the campus praying that God would cleanse me and give me strength to overcome my passions.

Now, as I look back on that serious young man I used to be, I am moved with compassion. I think he was unnecessarily guilty. There was no genuine lust in those library stacks. What I experienced was merely sexual recognition. I saw that she was attractive and knew that there was sexual potential between us. I was quite sure when I brushed her arm that she was not a man! But nothing sinful occurred. I did not really desire her or make any evil designs upon her. In fact, I behaved very responsibly toward her. I controlled my thoughts, spoke to her politely, and walked away.

But my poorly educated conscience was doing a number on me. Thinking myself to be entirely inclined toward evil, I was tortured by the power of my sexual awareness. I felt guilty of sin when no sin had been committed. Although I am thankful for the Christian instruction that I had received about the sinfulness of the human heart, I also believe that in some ways the instruction had not been balanced in the area of sexuality. I was wrongly coming to the conviction that every sexually interesting experience was sinful. I was developing a seriously unbalanced attitude toward my sexuality that would take many years to correct.

The most significant weakness in the church's teaching, I believe, has been in the failure to distinguish between sinful lust and normal sexual interest or fantasy that is not sinful. Many sincere and sensitive Christian people, inferring from the church's teaching that all their normal sexual interest or desire is lust, have wrongly condemned themselves. Furthermore, many people, feeling condemned already because of their thoughts, have simply given up in their attempts to live morally.

A conversation I had many years ago may serve as an illustration.

"If I've already thought it, I may as well do it. I'm guilty already. Isn't that right, preacher?"

I was a young seminary student working on a summer job in the steel mill when one of my workmates asked that question. I was not fully prepared to answer him.

"What do you mean?" I asked.

"Well, doesn't the Bible say that if you lust after a woman, you've already committed adultery?" he said.

Of course, he was right. Those are the words of Jesus in the Sermon on the Mount that were quoted above.

But was my friend right? Does it follow that if I've thought it in my heart, I'm as guilty as if I had actually done it already? Was that what Jesus meant to teach? Of course not! Can anyone imagine that Jesus was teaching that once an evil thought had entered the mind, we should not resist it? Indeed, part of Christian responsibility is to recognize when evil thoughts have entered the heart and to fight against those thoughts that would lead to evil actions. Sin conceived in the heart is certainly real sin, but is not as great an evil as the sin that issues in actual deeds.

Furthermore, as I look back at my friend at the steel mill, I certainly could not characterize him as an immoral man. He was a faithful husband and did not show himself to be given to immoral attitudes. He was not known for dirty talk or off-color stories. His work area was not plastered with pornographic pictures as were many of the others. He was a pretty decent man, actually. But I don't think that he thought he was a decent man. I believe that he was inwardly troubled about himself and he saw himself as sexually guiltworthy because he was too interested in sexual things.

Does every sexually interesting thought automatically qualify as sinful lust and, therefore, fall under the condemnation of Jesus? Emphatically not. But, if not, then what is lust? How can I distinguish between sexually oriented thoughts that are lustful and those that are innocent or appropriate?

Lust and Fantasy

First of all, not all sexually interesting or exciting thoughts are sinful. There are differences between lust and fantasy. *Fantasy* is a broad term referring to the whole range of things that the imagination can do with sexual thoughts. *Lust* is a more limited term referring to a particular form of sexual imagination. As Richard Foster says, "Although all lust involves sexual fantasy, not all sexual fantasies lead to lust."[1]

I am not necessarily guilty of sin just because I think about sex or view another person as sexually desirable. It is a natural, and quite healthy, part of being created in God's image to be able to think about what is sexually desirable. It is not sinful, for example, for a young girl to dream about being loved by a wonderful man one day. Neither is it wrong for a man to look at a woman with appreciation for her attractiveness and to recognize that she is sexually appealing, as I did in those library stacks many years ago. And it is not sinful for two people who are growing in love for each other to consider each other attractive and desirable, and to long for each other in sexual ways. These things are sexual imaginings, or fantasies, and are not in themselves sinful.

Lust, on the other hand, is preoccupation or obsession with sexual pleasure. It is what Foster calls "runaway, uncontrolled sexual passion."[2]

Lust goes beyond natural sexual interest and desire and looks upon others with the intention of using them merely for pleasure.

Lewis Smedes writes,

> It is foolish to identify every erotic feeling with lust. There is a sexual desire that feels like a lonely vacuum yearning to be filled, a longing for intimacy that broods unsettled in one's system. To identify this as lust is to brand every normal sexual need as adultery. Eros, the longing for personal fulfillment, must not be confused with lust, the untamed desire for another's body. Nor is every feeling of attraction toward an exciting person the spark of lust. . . . But attraction can become captivity; and when we have become captives of the thought, we have begun to lust. When the sense of excitement conceives a plan to use a person, when attraction turns into a scheme, we have crossed beyond erotic excitement into spiritual adultery. There need be no guilt when we have a sense of excitement and tension in the presence of a sexually stimulating person; but we also need to be alert to where that excitement can lead.[3]

Lust, then, is more than mere sexual interest or excitement. Lust is sexual desire that has gained control of the thoughts. Lust is interested only in making use of another person to satisfy its own sexual urges. Lust causes one person to view another not as a whole person but only in terms of sexual usefulness, merely as a sex object. When this attitude is in the heart, a person has committed adultery.

Appropriate Sexual Desire

But the human heart is also capable of entirely appropriate sexual desire. While it is true that all evil proceeds from the heart, it is also true that all good proceeds from the heart. And much of sexual desire is good. God has created man and woman to see each other as attractive and sexually desirable. When He created that mutual desire and desirability, He said it was good.

We need to remember that when a man and a woman begin to grow in sincere love for each other, something wonderful and good happens. True, whenever two people begin to be attracted to each other, there is always potential for the development of sinful lust, but the drawing together of two hearts is, in itself, a beautiful and marvelous thing. It is what the proverb described as the "the way of a man with a maiden" (Prov. 30:19 NIV), and it must be perceived as one of God's most special gifts.

The purpose of the Song of Solomon seems to be to celebrate this powerful and passionate sexual desire that may grow between a man and a woman. The book is wonderfully descriptive in its account of the sensuous desire felt by both the king and his bride. Passionate love for each other draws them to their wedding day, and that love is good.

Yet the love celebrated in the Song of Solomon is never portrayed as passion alone or as passion that has gained control. It is true passion, but it is passion guided by responsibility and restraint. Richard Foster describes it as "sensuality without licentiousness, passion without promiscuity, love without lust."[4]

Foster underlines the important balance between the intensity and the restraint of sexual love: "Alongside love's intensity we need to see love's restraint. There is no crude orgy here, no pawing and pounding. Love is too high, sex is too deep, for such leering and lusting."[5]

The love depicted in the Song of Solomon holds back on full expression until the wedding day. It is a love that controls desire rather than a love that is led by desire. It is God-given love, and it is good; but its goodness is preserved by the responsible restraint of the two lovers.

Here, it seems to me, is the key to understanding what is appropriate sexual desire and what is not. Attraction, desire, or passion alone is raw and dangerous. If two would-be lovers look into their hearts and see only desire, they must quickly be on their guard, for they may soon be devoured by the monster Lust. Powerful desires require spiritual guidance and responsible control. If the lovers look in their hearts and find that these, too, are present, they may rejoice that a growing love relationship is possible.

What Are Your Intentions?

In a previous era, a young man could not begin to court a young woman without first obtaining the permission of her father. If the young man requested the privilege of seeing her, her father was likely to ask him, "What are your intentions?" or "Are your intentions honorable?" These were, indeed, good questions, and one reason for our modern plague of foolish and careless sexual behavior among the young is that fathers no longer make any effort to take the measure of the young men who come calling on their girls.

But these are also good questions for single adults to ask themselves when they begin new relationships. Certainly, no relationship between a man and a woman will grow in a sexually healthy way unless they ask themselves and each other those questions about honorable intentions. It is especially important in our sexually supercharged times for people to seriously ponder their intentions. In our society there are so many messages of instant sexual gratification that even mature and generally responsible Christian people can easily find themselves hurrying into sexually powerful expressions before they have given any thought to what they are doing.

Talk Before Touch

We have all seen the sexual insanity of immediate physical intimacy being portrayed in today's books and movies. Two people meet, perhaps for the very first time, they exchange glances, they speak briefly about the weather or the stock market, and then, suddenly, BINGO, their clothes are off and they are in bed! Unbridled sexual passion is being presented to us as if it's the only possible option for total strangers. There is a better way.

That better way is the way of talk. The only possible way for a man and a woman to discover whether or not their relationship has the potential for healthy and happy growth is to talk to each other. The God-given ability to talk to each other, to share our inner selves, most distinguishes us from the animals and raises human sexuality above theirs. Only by talking openly and honestly can two people learn who they truly are together. And only by talking can they discover what forms of touch are appropriate ways of expressing their relationship.

The first principle I would apply to the development of healthy sexual relationships, then, is that *talk must always come before touch*. And there should be much talk, truly self-revealing talk, and talk that clearly expresses the intentions of the heart before there is any touch of an affectionate nature. People who jump into bed before they truly know each other and before they make the commitment of marriage violate God's holy law and their own inner integrity. They have physically expressed a kind of love that cannot possibly exist. Even persons who kiss on the first date have usually gone too far. Ordinarily, they do not know each other well enough to know if a kiss is an appropriate expression of their relationship.

The point is that self-sharing, not touch, should lead us in our relationships. We truly grow in relationships as we talk to each other honestly and responsibly. As we learn to share our true selves with each other, we can determine what forms of physical affection may properly express who we are together. Honest and responsible talk can protect us from merely using each other for physical and emotional pleasure and comfort.

As a relationship between two people grows and deepens, self-sharing talk will determine how much it has grown and in what ways it has grown. Physical expressions of affection, on the other hand, may easily lead into emotionally uncharted waters.

In chapter 5 I told you about two young friends of mine named Dan and Darlene. Thinking that they loved each other, they allowed physical affection to grow too rapidly. They began sleeping together only to discover that they were ahead of themselves. Darlene became possessive of Dan, and he didn't understand her. Dan was threatened by Darlene, and she couldn't understand that. Soon their relationship was over, and both were scarred.

What happened between Dan and Darlene illustrates what untold numbers of people discover somewhat regularly in our day. It is impossible for affectionate touch alone to tell us where we are in a relationship. Kissing, holding, petting, and having sexual intercourse have their special power to communicate strong feeling and to create a sense of deep intimacy. But they have no power at all to explain themselves. Physical touch, by itself, cannot reveal the true intentions of the heart. Without talk, therefore, we can never know what we are doing or what we should do.

Talk After Touch

It is also true that without talk we can never know what we have done. Every time two people begin to express their relationship with new forms of affection, they should talk about what is happening.

I will always remember the day after the first time I kissed the woman who is now my wife. We had known each other for over a year and had become good friends. We certainly knew that we cared deeply for each other as Christian brother and sister. We had shared our hearts in many mutually helpful ways. But when we first kissed good night, everything changed.

I recall that after we had parted that night, I was very confused by my feelings and by my concern over what she might be feeling. My heart was strongly drawn toward her. I knew that. But I was not at all sure of just what that meant. I knew that she was drawn toward me. But I did not know just what that meant, either. Talk time.

I called her the next day with a real case of nerves. After some small talk, I asked, "How are you feeling about last night?"

She responded, "I don't know. What do you think that was? Moonlight?"

"No," I said, "I don't think it was just moonlight, but I'm not sure just what I'm feeling."

Her next remark pointed the way to a responsible and growing relationship. "I think we need to talk," she said.

A simple good-night kiss may seem fairly low-key business in our day of sexual overkill, but a kiss has meaning. And unless its meaning is clearly understood by both people, there can be troubled waters just around the next bend. More than that, there are certain to be troubled waters ahead for those who do not carefully discuss the meaning of their growing relationship and, thereby, give guidance to that relationship.

When people fail to discuss the meaning of their physical expressions of touch, they run the risk of coming under the control of their mounting emotional desires. Soon, they may be led entirely by pleasurable sexual feelings, and feelings are blind. At that point many people fall prey to the lusts of their hearts and use each other only to satisfy their sexual desires without thought of what is best or honorable. Trouble!

Talk Creates Adjustment

Persons who talk honestly can also agree upon adjustments that need to be made in the way they express their feelings for each other. If one or both of them feel uncomfortable with the way in which they have touched each other, that needs to be stated. And the uncomfortable feeling must be respected. One who truly loves will always respect that the other feels uncomfortable and will be willing to make changes in the way they touch.

But here lies an especially tricky mine field for many people. Lovers are not always honest with each other about what they feel. In fact, many times they are not even honest with themselves. Because the desire to be loved intimately is so intense, and because such great pleasure and promise are in physical expressions of affection, people will often continue in behavior patterns with which they are not comfortable rather than risk weakening or losing the relationship.

I have seen this situation regularly in counseling settings. Shelley is a good example. She came to me soon after she discovered she was pregnant. She was a Christian girl of eighteen and had not yet told her parents. One of her good friends was encouraging her to have an abortion. At one point in the conversation I suggested that she and the baby's father should go to their parents with the problem.

Then she said something that startled me. "I don't want anything to do with him. I don't love him. I know I don't. I never really wanted to have sex with him."

"Shelley," I asked, "if you never wanted sex with him, how did it happen that you did have sex with him?"

"I don't know," she answered. "At first we would just kiss and hold each other, and that was really nice. But then he wanted to start doing other things. I never really wanted to do them, but I didn't want to lose him."

"Do you mean you were afraid that if you told him how you really felt, or if you asked him not to do these things, he would not stick around anymore?"

"Yes," she said. "It happened before with another boy I knew. He just never called me again. That's just the way guys are."

Shelley's story is sad but common. The desire to be loved often leads two people into forms of physical expression that are too intense for their relationship to bear. But many people don't know how to adjust their behavior to more properly fit their relationship. The risk of losing the relationship entirely can be very threatening, and many people will choose to say nothing rather than take that risk. The saddest part is that failure to talk honestly and to make necessary adjustments in a relationship will guarantee the continuing weakness of that relationship. And weak relationships have a tendency to depend on ever-increasing physical intensity to fill the vacuum.

For people who will not talk honestly, physical intimacy can become a terrible trap. Once the strong expressions of physical touch have begun, they can create a very pleasant illusion of real intimacy. People may feel joyful and exultant, alive and whole. It feels like intimacy, but it is not. Without honest and open talk about the meaning and direction of their relationship, they cannot develop true closeness. Meanwhile, their physical relationship may proceed rapidly, making their emotions all the more vulnerable to each other and talk more and more necessary.

When talk begins, however, it inevitably raises the questions of meaning and intention. What are we really doing together? Where are we headed? Such questions do not strengthen the sense of intimacy. In fact, they may create a threat. Perhaps this relationship is not all that we thought it was? Perhaps this person is only playing with me or using me? What do I really mean to my partner? Is this love or something else? If we do not talk, we cannot grow. But if we do talk, we may ruin what we have. The fear of loss often leads people to choose what feels safe rather than what could lead to real growth.

Many people have allowed the trap of physical intimacy to hold them in its grip while they cross one boundary after another until, finally, they find themselves in bed with a virtual stranger. Some people have even gotten married to virtual strangers. People who have had unhappy marriages often look back and recognize that they got married knowing almost nothing about how to be honest with each other.

Just a few weeks ago a woman spoke with me about her marriage and said, "I knew it was wrong when I was walking down the aisle on our wedding day. I can remember looking into my father's face as we walked along and crying. In my heart I was saying, 'This is wrong, wrong, wrong!' But I smiled at him as if to reassure him that I was just happy."

"Why were you so sure it was wrong?" I asked.

"Because we never really talked about anything. We just got all involved physically. You know, we thought we were in love, I guess."

"But you knew that you were not in love, didn't you?"

"I really did want to love Jim," she said, "but I was so full of questions about our relationship. I was just confused and afraid, I think."

"Did you ever talk about all your confusion?" I asked her.

"Not really," she answered. "Whenever I would start to say anything, he would avoid it. He would try to solve everything by saying he loved me or something. But he never really wanted to hear how scared I was. I guess I just thought I was dumb to be so scared, and everything was going to be all right."

This woman's story well illustrates the danger of allowing a relationship to proceed on a physical level without giving careful attention to the deeper level of the spirit. Sooner or later, the spirit of at least one person will challenge the nature of the relationship. Sadly, for untold numbers of people, it is far too late to turn back and build a healthy relationship of truly personal sharing.

On the other hand, persons who will honestly share their true thoughts and feelings from the beginning of a relationship are laying the foundation upon which they may build a strong and meaningful friendship—and, perhaps, even a marriage. As they continue to honestly discuss the meaning of their relationship, they will be able to determine what kinds of physical expressions most properly express that meaning.

They will also be able to make the adjustments necessary to keep their physical touching in step with the intentions of their hearts.

Petting Relationships

Questions about the propriety of petting are inextricably tied to the earlier questions about the intentions of the heart. We cannot determine what is appropriate behavior between a man and a woman merely by asking how they touch. We must know more than that. We must know who they are and what kind of relationship they have. Are they married? If so, they have the freedom to express themselves sexually in any way that is mutually respectful and agreeable. Are they virtual strangers on their first date? Then they would have no freedom at all for sexually expressive touch.

But what of people somewhere in between the first date and marriage (as many readers of this book will be)? The general answer is still the same: we must know who they are. Actually, a better way to say it is that *they* must know who they are. When it comes down to it, *they* will make their choices of behavior. To make wise choices about how they touch each other, they will have to make decisions about who they are together.

As a relationship assumes a truly loving and responsible character, it seems to me that more expressive forms of touching become appropriate. Two people just beginning to share a personal interest in each other may choose to hold hands or hug or kiss good night. As they become more sure of each other, and as they make significant statements of responsibility and commitment to each other, they may express themselves in stronger kissing, holding, or caressing. Persons who are engaged to be married and feel secure in their commitment to each other may appropriately choose to express their love in even more powerful ways. Of course by expressing themselves in stronger physical ways, they are taking certain risks. Physical expressions of affection may easily escalate into self-centered and lustful passions. In the name of "love" people may rationalize themselves into believing that anything goes and may choose behavior that is damaging or even destructive to the relationship. What begins as a pure and responsible sharing of hearts may, through carelessness, flame into immorality. Deepening forms of physical intimacy always require deepening personal commitment from both persons.

At this point Christian writers on morality differ widely. Lewis

Smedes, for example, sees petting as having positive potential for the growth and development of a personal relationship:

> Petting can be a delicately tuned means of mutual discovery. It need not be a cheap way of having the thrills of starting out toward intercourse without the derring-do to finish it. Petting can be an end in itself. It can be a process in which two people explore each other's feelings with no intention of having intercourse. Communication can take place that conveys personal closeness and sharing, with flexible but recognizable limits. It demands, of course, a sophisticated sense of appropriateness if it is not going to trap the players in a fondling game that goes beyond the implicit limits of their relationship. And this in turn calls for education of young people in responsible relationships. Thus petting is a tender route that *could* lead to coitus, but need not intend to go that far. It has many natural exits, each of which is marked by invisible signs that signal the place to stop, according to the amount of involvement that the two players have with each other as persons. It is not a cataract that carries partners over the falls of passion unless they halt the plunge and suffer the lesser fits of frustration. It is an adventure in personal understanding and intimacy that calls for control and discipline.[6]

Randy Alcorn, however, strongly opposes this line of reasoning. Quoting this same passage, he then comments,

> Such teaching provides an obvious moral justification for virtually any level of sexual stimulation outside of marriage. When wanting to become sexually involved, most young people will quickly conclude that they are indeed sophisticated and that theirs is a responsible relationship in which petting can be a tender and delicately tuned means of mutual discovery. For them, no doubt, petting can be an adventure in personal understanding, not a cheap way of having thrills. Indeed, if we bought this author's reasoning, any couple abstaining from petting would appear to be destined for a shallow relationship.[7]

Alcorn goes on to say,

> I do not agree that petting "has many natural exits, each of which is marked by invisible signs." What are invisible signs—are they like inaudible noises? How does one see an invisible sign, or know when he has seen one? Since petting is a physiological and emotional preparation for sexual intercourse, it will inevitably propel itself toward sexual intercourse. While there are exits, they are the very opposite of natural.[8]

Both men are worth listening to. Smedes places a much-needed emphasis on the fact that affectionate touch derives its meaning and purpose from the intentions of the heart. He argues persuasively, I think, that petting need not be defined narrowly as only a part of the inevitable process of preparation for intercourse. There are degrees and shades of meaning in sexual relationships, and they do not all lead inevitably to the bedroom. Petting can be responsible behavior if the two people involved will accept the responsibility of honest communication and discipline of their behavior.

Alcorn, on the other hand, believes it is unlikely that people will be able to develop such a degree of responsibility and self-control once they begin to touch each other in sexually excitable ways. He is unwilling to accept Smedes's concept that petting may have different levels of meaning depending upon the nature of people's relationships, and he defines petting strictly as "physiological and emotional preparation for sexual intercourse." He warns us that it is very easy to rationalize about our sexual behavior and to justify what is sinful.

My opinion is that Smedes is correct in teaching that the morality of petting depends on the nature of the personal relationship between two people and the degree of commitment they share. God has given only two absolute rules for how the unmarried may express growing love. He has commanded that intercourse must be reserved for the married alone, and He has commanded that we must not allow ourselves to be driven by lustful desire.

It seems to me, then, that it would be wrong to attempt to create rules going beyond what Scripture has said. We simply do not know enough to draw an absolute line to clearly demarcate responsible behavior for all couples. For those who are highly committed to each other and taking responsible steps toward marriage, there may be many acceptable expressions of affection that would be entirely out of place for those who are only dating and have no clear idea of where they are going.

But I do not wish to sweep Alcorn aside. He very wisely raises realistic cautions about the power of the passions to carry people well past their good intentions. It is true that many people do not have the maturity and strength of character required to carefully guide and control sexually expressive behavior once it has begun. People find ways to justify intense sexual behavior that is well beyond the limits of their commitment to each other.

Smedes also recognizes this point:

But if we avoid legalism, we should also avoid naivete. Petting is a risky game, and the players are not always responsible players. There is a wave of sheer lust and exploitation lurking in anyone—young or old—even though they mean to be responsible as Christians. It is as easy to exploit another person in petting as it is in intercourse; perhaps nowhere is a person more vulnerable than in petting. Hopes can be falsely aroused, and disguised lust can be mistaken for affection. A person's intense desire for love can translate the other person's lust into a message of genuine love. The rule of responsibility in petting requires a perception that not every person has, once his passions are aroused.[9]

How, then, can we balance our approach to sexually expressive touch outside marriage? How can we avoid both legalism and naivete? The answer is in learning to accept full responsibility for our relationships, knowing that we are free to express love only in ways that correspond to our willingness and ability to make honest commitments to each other. At the same time acceptance of responsibility means that we recognize our accountability to God and to each other to guard against any tendency to exploit each other for pleasure.

Richard Foster offers some helpful thoughts:

Responsible passion should be guided by one principle: *increased physical intimacy in a relationship should always be matched by increased commitment to that relationship. . . .* We build a solid foundation for love by moving toward commitment at the same rate we move toward physical intimacy. As intimacy grows, so does our commitment to each other. As our commitment grows, so does our intimacy. If our mutual commitment is shaky, we had better ease up on the intimacy.[10]

Foster then adds,

I would like to add to this two opinions of my own: if these are helpful, good; if not, forget them, for they are certainly not essential to the general principle. My first suggestion is this: since our purpose is to convey personal closeness and sharing without sexual intercourse, I think it would be wise to make the genitals and the woman's breasts off limits until marriage. These areas are just too explosive to be part of a mutual expression of affection and caring short of intercourse.

My second suggestion is that the engagement period not be too long—certainly not more than six months. By the time a couple reaches the point of engagement, they are entering levels of intimacy that should not be sustained for long without expression in sexual intercourse.[11]

Guidelines for Petting

I suggest three guidelines for thinking about petting relationships.

First, the morality of petting depends entirely upon the nature and depth of the relationship between two people. No outsider may make rules capable of giving others specific guidance for their conduct. Bearing in mind that God has forbidden relationships based merely on lust, and that sexual intercourse is always off-limits for the unmarried, each couple must examine and define their relationship and establish their own rules.

But intensity of feeling or desire is never a reliable test for measuring the strength of a relationship. Lovers must search their hearts for more than strong feelings. The only dependable method to measure the strength of a relationship is to ask what kind of promises, or commitments, the two people are willing to give to each other. Affectionate touch must communicate more than strong desires—it must communicate trustworthy promise as well.

Second, petting must never be allowed to lead a relationship. Pleasant touching has no capability of defining or explaining itself. Two people must talk about how they touch and why they are touching in the ways they are. They must require themselves to explain their actions and hold themselves accountable for their behavior. If at any point they discover that they have allowed their feelings to lead them into forms of touch too powerful for their relationship, they will have to back up and establish more responsible limits on the way in which they touch.

Personal accountability and self-control strengthen the relationship and add meaning to whatever forms of affection the two people choose. If I know that the person who is touching me is under control of herself and fully willing to be accountable to me, I am more assured that her touch may be trusted. To adapt an old phrase, her touch is her bond.

A couple having trouble with self-control in a petting relationship may find it helpful to make themselves accountable to someone else. Many churches and singles ministries have found that when dating couples willingly submit themselves to the counsel and guidance of a mature Christian friend or another couple, great strength may be added to their relationship. I knew of three dating couples who regularly got together to discuss their relationships and hold each other accountable. They all found the experience to be very helpful.

Third, petting, like all other human behavior, must be viewed as a part of our discipleship to Christ. All that we are and all that we have we owe to Him. He has called us to serve Him by doing whatever we do for the glory of God (1 Cor. 10:31). Sincere Christian people who are growing in a love relationship ought to see that the way in which they touch each other has potential to draw them closer to Christ or to drive them from Him.

I can think of two ways in which a petting relationship could weaken people in their relationship with the Lord.

1. If it violates the conscience. The biblical principle that "whatever is not from faith is sin" (Rom. 14:23) has application to the way in which lovers conduct themselves. There are areas of conduct in life in which God has not given specific instructions but has left us to the freedom of our consciences before Him. If we have honestly yielded ourselves to the teachings of His Word and have prayed for His guidance, and our consciences remain clear before God, we are free to serve Him as we choose in that area. Paul wrote, "Happy is he who does not condemn himself in what he approves" (Rom. 14:22).

But we must be honest. If we have been instructed by God's Word and have prayed for guidance, and our consciences trouble us about a specific behavior, Paul has a further instruction: "The man who has doubts is condemned if he [so conducts himself, because his conduct] is not from faith" (Rom. 14:23 NIV).

To contradict one's conscience is to sin against God. And in a relationship one must guard against violating his own conscience and causing the other person to violate her conscience. There is much potential in a petting relationship for sins against conscience. And two people involved in such a relationship must be very honest with each other about what their consciences are saying to them. Each one must also greatly respect the conscience of the other person. Another Scripture passage tells us clearly that in sexual matters "no one should take advantage of and defraud his brother" (1 Thess. 4:6).

2. If it becomes obsessive. It is also sinful for us to allow anything to become an all-consuming or controlling factor in our lives. Christians are called to live under the control of God's Holy Spirit and nothing else. Once again, Paul has a word for us: "All things are lawful for me, but I will not be brought under the power of any. . . . The body is not for sexual immorality but for the Lord, and the Lord for the body" (1 Cor. 6:12–13).

It is possible for two people to become so enthralled by the powerful feelings of a petting relationship that they actually come under its control. Petting then is no longer a meaningful expression of genuine love, but a lustful obsession. They no longer control it, but it has taken control of them. When this happens, other vital parts of their relationship become neglected or entirely ignored. Petting can become the main reason that they get together.

When petting becomes obsessional, it will crowd the Lord out of people's relationships and take center stage for itself. This, it seems to me, is the most significant concern of all in evaluating a petting relationship. Can the two people involved honestly say that the way in which they touch each other with affection draws them closer to the Lord they serve? Does it demonstrate to them that they are always under His control and aware of their accountability to Him? Or has it become a master over them, a kind of false god, drawing their hearts away from a central devotion to Christ?

1. Foster, *Money, Sex and Power,* p. 121.
2. Ibid.
3. Smedes, *Sex for Christians,* p. 210.
4. Foster, *Money, Sex and Power,* p. 95.
5. Ibid., p. 95.
6. Smedes, *Sex for Christians,* p. 151.
7. Randy Alcorn, *Christians in the Wake of the Sexual Revolution* (Portland, Oregon: Multnomah Press, 1985), p. 223.
8. Ibid., p. 224.
9. Smedes, *Sex for Christians,* p. 154.
10. Foster, *Money, Sex and Power,* p. 128.
11. Ibid., p. 130.

12

Masturbation

I have tried everything I know how to stop. For a long time I was so full of guilt and shame. I just thought I must be the most lustful person in the world. Sometimes I have just hated myself. I have prayed and prayed. I have tried exercise programs. I have eaten bland foods. Sometimes, I think that I've overcome it, then it comes back. Now I don't even try to quit. I guess I feel defeated, and certainly still feel guilty. But I really don't understand it. Why can't I get rid of the habit? Is it sin? It really is sin, isn't it?"

I will call this woman Margaret. She was attending a seminar where I was speaking and had asked me for a private session. We talked for a long time about her struggle with the habit of masturbation.

She is certainly not alone. Studies indicate that masturbation is almost universal among men and quite widespread among women. And it is also almost universally true that people do not know what to think about it. Many people, especially the young, experience deep feelings of guilt and self-condemnation. Others accept it as a normal part of life and a morally acceptable way to relieve physical and emotional tension. Christians are especially troubled by the fact that masturbation is almost always associated with sexual fantasies and that it can easily become obsessional.

Is Masturbation Sin?

Once again, we are considering something about which the Bible is silent. Therefore, we must be careful neither to condemn nor to approve the practice of masturbation categorically. The best answer to give to Mar garet's question is that masturbation is not always sinful or even sinful in itself, but because of its close association with lustful thoughts and its tendency to become obsessional, it can be sinful.

The key to understanding the moral character of masturbation is in determining the motives causing people to do it. There are numerous reasons why people masturbate; some are sinful, some are not, and others are real judgment calls.

Self-Discovery

Adolescents usually begin to masturbate as a normal part of the discovery of their own bodies' capabilities. Depending on what they have already learned about sex, they may bring some lust into the act, but they are more likely experimenting with what their bodies can do.

They are discovering that the genitals are capable of producing pleasant feelings, and they know instinctively that these feelings have something to do with being a man or a woman. Because they almost always discover it while alone, the discovery may be accompanied by feelings of uncertainty about themselves or even fear of abnormality. They will not usually go to their parents to ask for information about what they have discovered, which may make them even more restless or guilty.

I see no reason to condemn masturbation in these early times. Young people do not ordinarily begin to masturbate because they are motivated by evil desires; they are simply maturing. Parents need to be alert to the likelihood of the masturbation experience and ready to discuss it with their children in a healthy and compassionate way. Parents who possess the willingness (and the courage) to approach the topic with their children can provide an encouraging and steadying force as the children learn about their sexuality.

Dr. Smedes is helpful on this point:

The moral response to masturbation will be one of asking how we can help youngsters pass through this phase into a responsible heterosexual life. We will want to help them integrate this temporary activity, with all its unsatisfying after feelings, into their struggles toward mature and whole personhood. I think it is naive to suppose that we can rid youngsters of all uneasiness and shame connected with masturbation. But we can help them avoid getting into the compulsive rut of spiritual self-abuse. And the basic means that God has wondrously made available is the assurance of His grace, the confidence of His total and unconditional acceptance.[1]

Of course, the problem for the vast majority of young people is that they are not going to have assuring talks with their parents. They are not going to bring up the subject, and neither are their parents. In most cases, they will learn about the meaning of masturbation all by themselves. One can only encourage parents to swallow hard and dare to bring up the subject. Children may act embarrassed or indifferent, but it will be a considerable help for them to know that their parents would not condemn them for masturbation.

Growing Sexual Awareness

During the same general period of time in which youngsters discover that their genitals can be exciting, they also discover themselves. Along with the knowledge of what the body can do comes the whole range of thoughts and questions about what it means to be a man or a woman, including many questions about what sexual activity is actually like. Depending on the kind of information they have received about sexuality (whether positive, negative, or confused), young people begin to construct their view of themselves as sexual persons.

If young people have received generally positive signals about sexuality up until this time in life (if, for example, the parents are openly affectionate and happy with each other), they are most likely to view sex in a positive light. Gradually, they will learn to integrate the new information they receive about the body and their sexual potential into a healthy and balanced view of themselves. For these youngsters, it is most likely that masturbation, too, will eventually be understood in a balanced and healthy way. They will tend to see masturbation as one part of the body's growing up, only a temporary pointer toward mature sexual experience.

However, if young persons have received mostly negative information about sexuality or, worse, no information at all, their view of sexuality may become negative. For them, masturbation can become a deeply troubling source of guilt or fear. Youngsters who have learned that sex is evil or "nasty" may believe that masturbation is proof of their badness.

Dwight Carlson comments on the possible results of such an attitude: "It must be pointed out that many young people who have been taught that masturbation is sinful, in fact, spend more time struggling with destructive thoughts than many other individuals who do not view masturbation as sin."[2] A source of trouble for many people is that they were, in fact, taught that sexuality is basically evil. Many parents and other relatives (often owing to their own poor training) have sown the seeds of negative thinking and self-condemnation in children.

The mere fact that a youngster's family never talks about sex openly may cause him to sense that it is taboo. Therefore, while his maturing body is sending him interesting sexual signals, he is likely to feel an accompanying need to resist those signals. His resultant attitude toward sex can easily be that he desires it, fears it, and finds himself trying to ignore it all at the same time.

But whether or not their view of sexuality is healthy, it is inevitable that adolescent boys and girls will notice each other more and more, and that they will think about what it will be like to have a mature love relationship and, specifically, sexual intercourse. But since they do not yet have mature social relationships or legitimate opportunities for sexual involvement, this period of adolescent growth is often accompanied by increased masturbation.

This is especially true for a boy for at least three reasons. First, a boy is sexually stimulated by vision, and stimulating sights are abundant. Second, because a boy's genitals are external to the body, they are subject to stimulation by the rubbing of clothing, movement, and even temperature. Third, because his body is becoming active in producing semen, he will often experience physical tension, or pressure, in the genitals. For any of these reasons, a young man may experience genital stimulation, or even an erection, in the most awkward times. In such times, masturbation becomes a ready solution to an aggravating or embarrassing problem.

A young girl is much more inward about her sexuality. If she masturbates, it ordinarily begins with emotional and mental stimulation, not with visual or physical stimulation. An adolescent girl tends to be much more captivated by the thought of being loved. She reads love stories, watches love scenes, and listens to love songs, and she dreams wonderful dreams about what a sexual relationship with a man might be like. Such thoughts will sometimes lead to masturbation. Studies indicate, however, that girls generally do not masturbate as frequently as boys and often do not masturbate to orgasm.

To underscore an earlier point, it does not seem to me that the increased frequency of masturbation during the adolescent years is, in itself, an evil or even a danger. The process of sexual maturation quite naturally includes a new awareness and interest in the body and its functions as well as a growing desire to be loved by someone special. Neither the discovery of genital pleasure nor the mental fantasies accompanying this new awakening need necessarily be viewed as evil. Masturbation ought to be accepted as a part of the natural experimentation through which adolescents will go in their progress toward adulthood. It must be added that masturbation provides a safe form of genital and emotional release for those who are still in the process of developing a mature understanding of their sexuality.

Richard Foster comments on the positive aspect of masturbation:

> Masturbation does help compensate for the uneven development that many adolescents experience in their physical, emotional, and social maturation. Many teenagers are physically ready for sex far sooner than they are for social intimacy and the responsibilities of marriage. Masturbation provides a natural "safety valve" while nature is synchronizing growth in the various aspects of life.[3]

Although it would be a mistake to criticize or condemn masturbation in itself, it would also be a mistake to approve of masturbation as a normal part of growing up without saying anything further. The fact is that masturbation has the potential for becoming sinful behavior in certain cases.

Enslavement to Sexual Fantasies

The first way in which masturbation may become a sinful behavior is if it becomes habitual or obsessive. The danger is not in the physical act of masturbation, but in the gradual enslavement of the mind to lustful thinking. The more masturbation tends to become an obsessive thing, the more it becomes idolatrous.

Earlier, I discussed the primary Christian duty of guarding the mind from anything that would crowd the Lord from center stage in the thoughts. It is part of the first and greatest commandment to "love the Lord your God . . . with all your mind" (Mark 12:30). Mental self-discipline and self-control are parts of the Christian life, and anything that tends to gain control of the thought life challenges the rule of Christ. Serious Christians will not want their minds to be controlled by sexual fantasies and desires.

An essential part of healthy sexual growth is to keep sexual fantasies in a balanced perspective. As has been stated, sexual fantasies have a proper place in normal human development. It is not sinful, in itself, to imagine or to notice what is sexually desirable. Nor is it sinful to dream of being loved by a wonderful and beautiful person. But it would be sinful to cultivate and magnify sexual desire by yielding oneself to its every call and thereby allowing it to gain control of one's behavior. Masturbation can become a form of doing just that.

Keeping a balanced perspective in one's thought life requires a balanced diet of sexual and spiritual information, but most adolescents do not have that. They usually do not view themselves as "going through a phase" that their parents and most other adults have gone through. They are unable, therefore, to view their inner sexual struggle with any lightness at all. It is serious to them, often overpoweringly so. Sex matters to them perhaps like nothing else has ever mattered before.

Add to this the fact that in most cases adolescents do not enjoy the privilege of open and understanding discussion of sexual matters with a mature person, and you have young persons with an increasing sense of loneliness in regard to sexuality. Loneliness may increase the need for them to find some form of personal, private expression of their sexuality. Masturbation easily becomes such an outlet.

Another factor—a sense of guilt—may add to the possibility that masturbation become obsessive behavior. Adolescents are generally possessed by many insecurities and uncertainties about themselves simply because they are immature. Are they OK or not OK? Are they normal or abnormal? Are they acceptable or not? Will they ever find a role in life? These unsettled feelings about themselves may be experienced as a vague and unspecified guiltiness. If they have received poor information about sexuality, they may transfer this general, nonspecific feeling of guiltiness to the more concrete area of their interest in sex.

Unresolved guilt can drive persons into a sense of isolation and even desperation from which they search for release. Once again, masturbation may serve as a release, but it cannot solve the inner, emotional conflicts. It may only add to the sense of guilt, thus perpetuating a behavioral cycle. Dr. Smedes suggests that in such cases masturbation may actually become a form of subconscious self-punishment:

> They need something specific on which to fasten their feelings, and, since their guilt feelings are already fuzzily related to uneasiness about their sexuality, what better peg is there to hang their guilt feelings on than

masturbation? They already feel somewhat empty and unsatisfied about masturbation; and it is very easy to translate this feeling into guilt. So they masturbate and punish themselves afterward with cruel self-accusations.[4]

But we are only theorizing here. Whatever validity may lie in linking such factors as sexual immaturity, loneliness, and guilt feelings, there is another part to the problem, and that is of the lust of the heart. There is such as thing as prurient interest in sex, and to a degree, it resides in every human breast. It is possible to look upon sexuality as merely a way to have physical pleasure. On this level masturbation can become simply a means of enjoying sexual fantasy and genital stimulation for their own sake. If this happens, the individual is yielding to imagination and appetite alone and is divorcing genital sexual feeling from its proper spiritual and inter-personal context.

There is a considerable spiritual danger here. To enjoy sexual fantasy for its own sake and to allow its every occurrence to drive one to self-stimulating genital release is a form of both idolatry and spiritual and mental adultery. It is idolatry because it permits something other than the true and living God to control one's behavior. It is adultery because it allows the mind to focus on members of the opposite sex as mere sex objects that exist only for one's sexual pleasure.

Pornography

The multimillion dollar industry of pornography caters to prurient sexual interests. Books, magazines, recordings, and videos portraying people in various types of adventurous sexual involvement abound. Such material is readily available to the young and has become an intrinsic part of the sexual miseducation of millions of people in our society. It seems to me that using this material as a stimulus and an aid in masturbation is plainly sinful behavior.

Although a young person's first interest in pornographic material may be out of curiosity, many have discovered that an interest in pornography can become an obsession in itself. When it does, it is almost inevitably linked with the practice of masturbation. For many people, using stimulating pornographic materials for the purpose of masturbation becomes a chaining habit that lasts much longer than adolescence, sometimes continuing even in marriage.

The spiritual danger in pornography is primarily in its power to lock the mind into unrealistic fantasy. The world of pornography appeals largely on this basis—it presents as real things that are not. With special camera and art techniques it is able to create pictures of the human body that far transcend what the ordinary body looks like. And the written word can create mental pictures far beyond the power of the camera and art. The result can be that the attractiveness of real human beings and realistic sexual relationships fade in comparison.

The songwriter Paul Simon, in his song "Kodachrome," commented on the transcendence of sexual fantasy over real people. The song contains a line in which he envisions taking all the girls he had known when he was single and bringing them together for one night. Even then, he suggests that they could never do for him what his imagination could do. The closing line says it all, "Everything looks worse in black and white."

When people are victimized by believing in an unreal world of sexual perfections, real people will be less and less attractive and real relationships less and less desirable to them. As Simon says, nothing can match the imagination, and everything looks worse in black and white. For such people, masturbation, assisted by the artificial props of pornography, can become spiritual bondage and idolatry. Their minds can be imprisoned by unreal and unreachable fantasies that they vainly seek to achieve through compulsive masturbation.

Self-Centeredness and Depersonalization

A second potential evil in the habit of masturbation lies in its basic self-centeredness. Because its focus is on personal pleasure, the purpose of masturbation is quite different from the purpose of a wholesome sexual relationship. In healthy sexual relationships people seek to grow by extending themselves into each other's whole lives. Physical sexual touch and intercourse are parts of that self-extension. In healthy relationships people seek to give pleasure and to share pleasure.

But in masturbation, the only emphasis is on gaining pleasure for oneself. The focus is on oneself, one's feelings, one's orgasm, and nothing else. A conversation I once had may illustrate how misdirected this focus can be.

"I never want anything to do with any man again," said a woman I will call Sandy.

"And why not?" I asked.

"Because there is no man anywhere who can do for me what I am able to do for myself at home alone," she replied.

"Are you talking about masturbation?" I inquired.

"Yes," she snapped at me. "I've had a lot of men, and I've never had one who knew how to give me the feelings I can give myself."

"Well, of course," I said.

"What do you mean?" she asked.

"I mean that when you masturbate, the only person you have to think about is yourself. You know what feels good to you, and you can do it just the way you want it done. You don't have to bother with communicating your needs to another person. So, of course, it's easier to create those feelings for yourself. But is that all sex is, just your feelings?"

She looked a little puzzled and said, "I don't know what you're saying."

"I'm saying that sex has to do with a lot more than just achieving your own orgasmic pleasure. Sex is supposed to be about two people seeking to share themselves with each other in a way that creates pleasure for both. And to do that, people have to be considerate of each other, they have to talk to each other about what feels good and what doesn't, and they have to be patient with each other while they learn."

"That sounds nice," she said, "but where I've been, it has never happened, and I really don't expect that it ever will."

Undoubtedly, some of her frustrations were legitimate. Her relationships had not been rewarding sexually, and very possibly a large part of the problem had to do with her partners' lack of sexual skills. At any rate, her focus had begun to grow inward so that she was thinking basically in a self-centered way. Her only concern was what felt good to her, and in her judgment masturbation was superior to a sexual relationship with a man.

It is not wrong to seek the reward of pleasure where pleasure is a proper goal, and certainly, one goal of healthy sexuality is receiving pleasure in a relationship. But this woman was allowing her pleasure to become the primary focus in her thinking about sex. Therefore, she was willing to substitute the lonely sexual experience of masturbation for the hard work and rewards of an actual relationship.

To use masturbation as a substitute for relationships is to lower sexuality to the nonpersonal level. It may be said that masturbation is not really sexual activity at all because only one person is involved. Sexual activity requires partners because it requires the giving and receiving of pleasure.

J. I. Packer succinctly says, "Sex is for relationships, not ego trips."[6] John White, in *Eros Defiled,* also comments on the depersonalizing effect of masturbation:

> Masturbation is autostimulation, not sexual stimulation by another person. It is an intrapersonal not an interpersonal affair. Its defect lies at this very point: it takes what was meant to be a powerful urge encouraging a close personal relationship but aborts it. That which was meant to be shared is squandered in solitude.[7]

This depersonalizing tendency, perhaps more than any other aspect of masturbation, makes it dangerous to personal and spiritual health. Sexuality, as God intends it, is the whole-life sharing of two persons in both body and soul. In a healthy sexual relationship, physical sexual touch and the act of intercourse are properly placed within the context of personal sharing, responsibility, and commitment.

But masturbation, if it becomes obsessive, can remove physical genital pleasure from the context of those personal qualities altogether. The resultant depersonalization can affect persons' attitudes toward themselves and their attitudes toward others. First, they may interpret their sexual desires not as the God-given urge toward wholeness in relationship but merely as a genital need. Second, they may, as a consequence, tend to view other members of the opposite sex merely as sex objects who have the potential to serve their need for genital pleasure. This is the essence of adultery—to forsake God's design for healthy and responsible sexuality, and to use others for one's own pleasure. For these individuals, sexual wholeness and sexual fulfillment are impossible.

Single Again and So Alone

The people at our Fresh Start programs who are concerned about masturbation are not adolescents struggling with the first steps toward sexual understanding and growth. Neither are they usually people who are spiritually undisciplined and enslaved to their lusts. Ordinarily, they are serious Christians seeking to serve the Lord, and until their divorce experience, they were generally balanced and in control of themselves sexually. A combination of heartbreak and loneliness seems to have driven them to masturbation. Jeff's story is especially interesting.

"Tom, I never had a problem like this before. I mean not even when I was a teenager. You know, I masturbated some. I guess all boys did. But it wasn't a real habit. I pretty much had control of my passions for several years before Jackie and I got married."

"What about while you were married?" I asked. "Were there times when you were frustrated and would masturbate?"

"A couple of times when Jackie was pregnant, and I knew it would not be good for her to have intercourse. But it's just never been a problem for me. I guess I'm not as highly sexed as some guys, at least not until now. Now it's almost a daily problem. I just can't get her off my mind. And when I do masturbate, I think of her. I mean, no pornography or anything like that. Usually, I take Jackie's picture and just lay it on the pillow next to me. I miss her so much."

Jeff turned his head away and sobbed. His anguish touched me deeply because I had been where he was, and I understood.

There have been others, both men and women, who have told me of masturbating after a divorce or the death of a spouse in an effort to direct their sexual energies toward the absent loved one. Often they experience the need for sexual release much more intensely than they did while married. They are broken and lonely and in need of comfort. But they are not interested in developing new relationships, and they are usually not emotionally ready for another relationship. So they masturbate and fantasize about the former mate.

Sometimes these people are also keenly aware of their sexual vulnerability and the dangers of immorality, and they view masturbation as a kind of "safety valve" for the release of tension. For them, masturbation is, at least for a time, a morally wiser choice than a new relationship. Yet, masturbation is still a disturbing matter for them. They feel like teenagers again, they worry that they are too interested in sex, and they doubt the validity of their "safety valve" theory. They wonder what God thinks of them.

I have nothing but compassion for these people. They are in many ways a lot like teenagers again. They are unsure of their identity; they doubt their goodness; they fear the inability to develop a truly mature relationship. Yet, they are sexually mature and sexually experienced people (in this they are quite different from teenagers). In addition, the experience of rejection and failure has caused then to retreat inside themselves to nurse their wounds. It is no surprise that they would seek some release in masturbation.

Generally, these people need the same counsel that should be given to adolescents. Masturbation should not be viewed as a great moral failure; rather, it is a normal part of the emotional adjustment needed by people going through a deeply stressful transition in life. For healthy persons, masturbation will be a temporary matter and will decrease in frequency as emotional and social balance return to their lives. In time, the majority will recognize that there is no point in clinging to fantasies about the former mate. As the stress of their lives subsides, they will also find that they are not so intensely focused on sexual need.

However, the same spiritual dangers that were mentioned earlier apply to those who have been divorced or bereaved. Times of vulnerability are times of personal weakness, and it is easy to fall into sinful attitudes and behavior patterns in such times. If a person continues to masturbate frequently after a reasonable period of time (although it would be a mistake to arbitrarily set a time limit), the behavior may have become obsessive. In such cases it is possible for the individual to fall into the mental patterns of enslavement to lust and a self-centered fixation on genital release. Such dangers exist for everyone.

People who fear that they have fallen into obsessive masturbation should seek the encouragement of a solid Christian counselor. Sometimes all that is needed is an encouraging and understanding friend who can offer the balanced guidance of the Scriptures in a compassionate and caring way.

The Obsession to Stop

One final encouragement needs to be given. The disproportionate sense of guilt often accompanying masturbation may lead sensitive Christian people to an intense, even obsessive, desire to stop. Richard Foster has a useful statement on this problem:

> Obsessive masturbation is spiritually dangerous. But we must also be aware of the opposite obsession—the obsession to quit. This obsession is especially painful because one failure can cast a person into despair. It becomes a desperate, all-or-nothing situation. And this is sad, because it is really unnecessary. We do not need to put people into impossible either/or binds. What we are after is control, balance, perspective.[8]

Another encouraging word comes from Randy Alcorn:

We only add to "the problem" when we act as if someone's spirituality is all wrapped up in the issue of masturbation. Such attitudes result in more pressure and magnified guilt and lead to continuous failure and a deeper sense of inadequacy and despair. The person involved often gives up and is driven to the very behavior he is being condemned for.[9]

These men deliver wise counsel to persons possessed by the need to break the masturbation habit. Indeed, it is possible to become so intensely focused on a supposed sin that we develop a kind of spiritual tunnel vision that in turn, can prevent us from seeing the whole picture as God sees it.

We need a realistic sense of the grace of God to imperfect people. It is true that God hates all sin. That is plainly taught in Scripture. But it is also true that God loves sinners, and He has made the supreme sacrifice of giving up His own Son, Jesus, to bear the guilt of human sin on the cross. Through faith in Him we are promised that God will receive us as His own children "just as we are." We must not refuse the grace of God by wrongly focusing on one special sin and considering it too great for God to handle.

There are many pockets of evil in every Christian life, and God sees them all. But God's process of correcting our sinful ways is the patient and loving process of a compassionate Father who dearly loves His weak children. Persons obsessed with correcting some evil in their lives, such as masturbation, need to recognize that God may not be as obsessed with the problem as they are.

On this issue, John White helpfully remarks,

God has His own program for reshaping our lives. No exact hierarchy of sins or virtues is laid down in Scripture though general principles can be observed. In dealing with you and me God is doing what we do ourselves when we try to untangle a knotted tangle of string. Certain knots have to wait until other tangles are straightened.[10]

In the end the correction of the habit of masturbation will occur in the same way that any spiritual growth occurs: by believing God. We need to come to Him always in faith, knowing that His love is greater than our sins. In prayer we need to ask Him to take away our sinful habits as we perceive them. But we need to remember Dr. White's counsel as well— "certain knots have to wait until other tangles are straightened."

God knows our sins better than we do, and He knows His plan for our complete restoration and renewal. Perhaps persons who are focused on the need to overcome masturbation are failing to see something else in their lives that God wants them to focus on first. Possibly they need a more balanced understanding of the meaning and purpose of their sexuality. Maybe they need to develop stronger relational skills and build some true friendships. Perhaps they just need the assurance that in Christ they are truly accepted by God. Whatever their specific inner need, if they will sincerely present their hearts to Him and ask for His inner strength, He will give it to them; step by step, in His timing, they will grow into the people He wants them to be.

1. Smedes, *Sex for Christians,* p. 164.

2. Dwight Carlson, in *Sex and the Single Christian: Candid Conversations,* ed. Barry Colman (Ventura, California: Regal Books, 1985), p. 75.

3. Foster, *Money, Sex and Power,* p. 125.

4. Smedes, *Sex for Christians,* p. 163.

5. Paul Simon in "There Goes Rhymin' Simon" (New York: Charing Cross Music, 1973), p. 4.

6. J. I. Packer, *I Want to Be a Christian* (Wheaton, Illinois: Tyndale House Publishers, 1982), p. 293.

7. John White, *Eros Defiled: The Christian and Sexual Sin* (Downers Grove, Illinois: Inter-Varsity Press, 1977), p. 37.

8. Foster, *Money, Sex and Power,* p. 126.

9. Alcorn, *Christians in the Wake of the Sexual Revolution,* p. 217.

10. White, *Eros Defiled,* p. 44.

Therefore, I urge you, brothers, in view of God's mercy, to offer your bodies as living sacrifices, holy and pleasing to God—this is your spiritual act of worship. Do not conform any longer to the pattern of this world, but be transformed by the renewing of your mind. Then you will be able to test and approve what God's will is—His good, pleasing and perfect will (Rom. 12:1–2 NIV).

M any of the people who come to our Fresh Start seminars have been lied to, some for many years. They are furious about it, and rightly so. Because they have believed someone's lies, usually a former spouse, they feel they have been fools. They feel cheated out of parts of their very lives. They feel fouled and besmeared. For these reasons they are often highly skeptical. Some are determined never to trust anyone again.

But there is a lie that many people love to believe. It is the oldest lie of all. It is The Lie told by the serpent in the Garden of Eden when he tempted Eve. It has several parts, but its essence is that it is possible for men and women to have a full and happy life without worshiping the true God above all other things.

The serpent's lie told Eve that worshiping and obeying God were really unnecessary. All that was really needed for nurture, for pleasure, and for wisdom was to reach out and choose for oneself what God had forbidden. It was obvious that the forbidden fruit was "good for food, that it was pleasant to the eyes, and . . . desirable to make one wise" (Gen. 3:6).

The choice to believe the serpent's lie resulted in our first parents being cast out of God's Garden of blessing, and the whole human race was plunged into the darkness of life (if, indeed, it can be called life) without God. Believing that God has lied to them, millions reach out each day for those things God has forbidden, convinced that disobedience is wisdom and that sin is good.

One form of believing The Lie is in believing that uninhibited sexual intimacy outside marriage is a good thing. Our world shouts the message at us. Sex need not mean commitment for life! Sex may rightly mean whatever two consenting adults choose it to mean! Promiscuity is exciting and smart! Virginity is a mark of immaturity! Single people who do not have sex regularly are probably mentally ill! Everybody (everybody who is normal) is doing it! You should do it, too!

When people choose to doubt and disobey God, they choose to believe and obey something else in His place. They replace God with their makeshift false gods and bow before them daily. And they die. This was part of God's warning to Adam and Eve in the garden: "In the day that you eat of it you shall surely die" (Gen. 2:17).

It will kill you to turn away from God and worship something else. It will be a slow and almost unnoticeable death at first. At first, it will not seem like death at all. At first, it will feel like living, like really living. But it will be death all the same. Gradually, it will draw the deep joy of life out of your very soul. Bit by bit, little by little, you will find yourself growing experienced in the spiritual death of The Lie. At first, the pleasure will seem to disappear. You will scramble to find other ways of pleasure, but soon you will find little pleasure at all. Then skepticism will enter, eating away at your very ability to believe that anything is really good.

Finally you will be bitter, wholly and thoroughly bitter. You will know that you have been lied to, that you have been cheated in life. But by then you will be so convinced of the truth of The Lie that you will not turn back to God. Instead, you will cling all the more determinedly to The Great Lie as daily it robs you of life itself. In the end your life will be over on this earth, and you will not know God. But still you will not change. You will face physical death and the terror of eternity believing The Great Lie and blaming God for all your bitterness.

The cruel bondage of The Lie is nowhere more evident than in the commitment of our age to sexual "freedom." Even professing Christians, in large numbers, have fallen prey to the sexual life-style of the world. Christians are victimized by the overtly sexual clothing styles, the subtly sexual overtones of advertising, the suggestiveness of modern humor and music, and the blatant advocation of sexual looseness portrayed in nearly all literature, movies, and television shows. It is easy to believe that "everybody" else is doing it and that we may as well do it, too.

But the Scriptures call us to the truth. Instead of conforming to the world around us, Paul urges us to become transformed by the renewing of our minds. God wants us to cleanse and renovate our minds with His truth, and that includes our thinking about sexual things. And the result of right thinking will be right living. The proof that our minds are being transformed will be seen in what we actually do with our bodies.

If we believe God, we will present our bodies to Him, willingly making whatever sacrifice that may require. This is spiritual worship—to recognize who God is, to believe Him, and to give Him our bodies. This is what we should expect. It is so in the world around us. Generally, we can tell what a man believes to be important by where he takes his body and by what he does with it. We discover who our gods are by examining the life-style of our bodies. If we love and worship the true God, we will give ourselves to Him.

Once after I had lectured on sexuality and singleness a woman said, "If I do what God wants me to do, I may never have intercourse again."

Of course, she was right. She could not know the future, but she feared the possible consequences of a life of obedience to God. She knew that a life of serving God would require her to be sexually obedient, and she feared that such a life would be dull and unrewarding. She was in the grip of The Lie. She had become convinced of the goodness, the pleasure, and the wisdom of a sexually disobedient life-style. Apart from the freedom to have sexual intercourse, whether she was married or not, she doubted that life could be good. She was struggling with a choice of gods.

In the end, the only real question in life is, Who is God? Who is the real source of life and blessing for mankind? The Lord God who created us, or something else, some supposed good thing that God is withholding from us? Each of us must answer that question. Is it better to worship and obey God or to worship and obey some other master?

Christian singles need to accept God's truth about their sexuality. They need to believe God when He says that the full expression of their sexuality belongs only within the committed love and promise of marriage. They need to recognize that sexual fulfillment is not the same thing as genital activity. They need to grow in their ability to build meaningful and satisfying friendships with both men and women without falling into the traps of sensuality. And they need to discover the rewards of living by faith in the goodness of God who alone is able to fill their lives with deep peace and joy whether they marry or not.

People who decide to believe and do the will of God will discover something. They will find that the will of God is good and pleasing and perfect. Those were the very things that the serpent promised Eve as her reward if she turned away from God's will. The fruit was perceived as good and pleasant and "perfect" for making her wise. But he lied. Only God's way is good, pleasing, and perfect. Sexual disobedience, or any other kind of disobedience, will in the end corrupt, disappoint, and destroy true life. Only a life of faith and obedience to God's truth produces spiritual wholeness and health. It is good, pleasant, and perfect.

Earlier I spoke of a woman who became angry with my teaching on submitting our sexuality to God's will. Several years later, she wrote a letter to me describing some of the subsequent changes that took place in her life. I don't have the letter any more and don't even remember the woman's name, but here is a partial reconstruction of what that letter said:

Dear Tom,

I don't know if you will remember me, but I spoke to you at the retreat in . . . about living the Christian single life and not being sexually active. I was really angry with your approach and thought you were totally out in left field. Today, I want to thank you for saying what you did.

I went home and fought what you had said for weeks, even months. I wished I had never heard you speak. I continued to date lots of men, and I was usually sexually active. But, you were right. More and more I found no real pleasure in what I was doing. Most of the men only wanted physical sex, and when one of them wanted a more committed relationship with me, I discovered that I had no ability to be committed to him.

I finally realized that I was having no fun at all, that even though I was sexually active I had no inner peace. I remembered what you had said, and I borrowed your tapes from a friend of mine who had also been at. . . .

This time around you made a lot more sense. When I was finished with the tapes I asked God to forgive me for my foolishness and disobedience and teach me how to live my life for Him. I felt a little dumb and sceptical, but it was amazing how I began to change. After a few weeks a new kind of quiet seemed to be growing in my life. It's been three months now since I've had sex with anyone, and I'm feeling stronger and happier than I've felt in years. Jesus Christ is my Lord, and I love Him for cleaning up my act and filling my empty heart with His love.

Thank you for being willing to stand up and speak the truth for our Lord. It's just like you said. God's way is good, pleasing, and perfect. I know. Keep telling it like it is.

In a time of widespread false worship a servant of God named Elijah publicly challenged four hundred and fifty prophets of the false god called Baal. He said, "God is God, Baal is not." He dared them to hold a public contest of worship. They would build an altar of sacrifice and pray to their god, and Elijah would pray to the Lord, the living God of Israel. The one who answered by sending fire from heaven to consume the sacrifice would be declared the true God.

Elijah challenged the people of Israel with these words, "How long will you falter between two opinions? If the LORD is God, follow Him; but if Baal, then follow him" (1 Kings 18:21).

All day long the prophets of Baal prayed for fire. They danced ritual dances. They shouted in desperation. They even slashed themselves with swords and spears. But nothing happened. No one answered them. Baal, you see, cannot hear.

Then Elijah asked for large jars of water to be poured on the sacrifice. The people doused the altar and the sacrifice three times with water. Then Elijah prayed, and the Lord heard. The fire of God fell and consumed the sacrifice, the altar, and even the water in the ditch. When the people saw what happened, they fell prostrate before the Lord and worshiped, saying, "The LORD, He is God! The LORD, He is God!" (v. 39).

I tell this story to call Christian singles to a life of faith and courage like that of Elijah. There was only one of him, and there were four hundred and fifty of the false prophets of Baal. But Elijah was right. The Lord is the only true God. The Lord alone deserves our faith and obedience. One man who believed the truth and had the courage to challenge falseness was able to turn many hearts back to Him.

Our society needs Christian single people who have the courage of Elijah in the face of the prophets of sexual falseness. We appear to be outnumbered, much like Elijah was. But we are right, and the sex-crazed, sex-worshiping society around us is wrong. Sexual fulfillment and wholeness are not to be found in the slavish devotion to passion and genital sex that our society so widely accepts. Man does not live by genital sex alone. Fulfillment in sexual matters, as in all of life, is the gift of God, and it is given only to those who love Him first and follow His rules. But we need more Elijahs to say so.

After several years of speaking on the subject of sexuality, I am discovering that a great many in our society are following the prophets of sexual "freedom" simply because they have heard no other message. Probably the two most frequent comments that I hear in response to my talks on single sexuality are, "How I wish someone had said these things to me years ago," and "This is what I always thought I believed; it is such an encouragement to hear someone say these things."

I am more convinced than ever that our world needs Christian teaching on sexual morality. But more than that, our world needs to know the God of grace who has looked upon the world with compassion and mercy and has sent His Son, Jesus, to pay the penalty for sin and grant forgiveness to those who trust in Him. But the world is not going to believe the Christian approach to morality, or the good news about Jesus, unless the world sees some Christian people whose lives demonstrate that God's will is good, pleasing, and perfect.

In bringing this book to a close, I want to suggest three ways in which Christian singles can respond to God's call to sexual purity and fulfillment and become a positive sexual influence in our sexually confused times.

1. Make a personal decision to commit your life to Christ. Ask Him to forgive and cleanse you of any sexual sin that you may have committed, and go forward with your life believing that His forgiveness is real. Also, accept the life of celibacy without reservation as long as you remain single. But keep striving to develop your sexuality in responsible Christian friendships with friends of both sexes. Grow wisely, grow carefully, but grow.

2. If you have children, share with them a wholesome, balanced view of sexuality. Be sure they hear that sexuality is God's wonderful gift to men and women, that it is a part of His likeness imprinted on our nature. Help them to know that they need not be ashamed of their interest in sex. If you have been divorced, it is especially important that you speak well of marriage. They need to believe that marriage, as God has planned it, is a wonderful estate. And do all that is in your power to help them understand why God reserves sexual intercourse for marriage alone. You cannot make their choices for them, but you can provide them with sound information, a good example, and a compassionate, understanding attitude. And pray for your kids. (See Appendix.)

3. Display to the world that the Christian approach to sexuality is the only way to real sexual freedom. Let it be known that you serve the Lord Christ, and that His mercies have cleansed and healed your life. You don't have to be annoying or obnoxious about it, but as the subject comes up, let others see by your attitude and style of life that you respect the opposite sex, that you willingly embrace a life of sexual purity and self-control, and that the will of God is good, pleasing, and perfect. There may be four hundred and fifty of them and only one of you. But if you are serving Christ with your life, you're right. Christ has used one servant in the face of four hundred and fifty before, and He can do it again.

Golly!
A Bedtime Story
for Parents

S ex began to fascinate me about the same time that it began to confuse me. But whenever it began, it grew steadily during my teenage years (and ever since, honestly) both in its fascination and in its confusion. I don't suppose I was much different from any boy who grew up in the forties or fifties. I was overwhelmed by the marvelous development of my sexuality, and yet I felt locked up in regard to sex.

Sex filled me with feelings of promise and foreboding. Something deep inside kept shouting about sex. It was a wonderful and exciting reality, that sexuality of mine. Yet no one talked about it at our house, and I felt that it was somehow a mistake on my part to be so entranced by it. In short, sex made me feel bad. In addition, feeling bad led to feeling guilty, because it isn't quite true that no one ever talked about sex around our house. Now and then it was mentioned, but when it was mentioned one had the feeling that it was a very nasty thing to talk about, and so I felt good *and* bad.

At any rate, there came a time in my mature years—after I had learned all the truths about sex (just about)—that I decided I was going to be very honest about it with all my children. They would not grow up in ignorance as I had, I vowed to myself. As soon as they began to show any interest in sex, I would stride forward in the interest of truth and tell what I knew. I was very coura-geous.

The great day came all too soon.

When that great day arrived, my son was eight. Eight! I suppose I had anticipated that he would be sixteen, or at least ten (double figures of some kind would have helped), but he was only eight, and he had already been asking for some time. His mother was about to have our third child, and our son had become increasingly interested in the process by which the new baby was being produced.

Of course, since he already had one sister who was then four, our inquisitive little eight-year-old had already been through basic training. That is to say, he knew about the stork myth, and he had felt Mommy's jumping tummy four years earlier. Now, however, he was ready for the big stuff.

It had begun during the first months of pregnancy. His mother and I had explained that there was soon to be a new baby. God was already making the baby grow inside Mommy. That was good news, and both brother and sister greeted it with awe and delight. I had later seized the opportunity to present our son with a very helpful illustrated book depicting the journey of the sperm to the egg cell, the mystery of fertilization, the nine-month gestation, and birth itself. I was really quite pleased with myself for having found the book and was feeling rather content until one day the inevitable question came.

It was at dinnertime one evening, and the talk had been vague and general. Then our little scientist said, "Daddy, there's something I don't understand."

"What's that?" I queried.

"Well, I know about the sperm and the egg . . ."

Uh-oh, I thought.

"But I guess I don't know how the sperm gets in there."

"Oh," I said.

It really seemed very quiet for a moment or two. I didn't look at my wife as I remember. I can't really explain what I thought, and if I didn't believe that most of you could identify with me, I'd be a bit embarrassed to tell you what I did. I avoided it.

"Well, Son, I'll explain that to you sometime," I promised. Then we continued to eat.

He didn't ask again, and I certainly didn't bring it up. Well, after all, it was mealtime, and his little sister was present, and she was only four! (I suppose thorough honesty would require me to admit that she certainly seemed to understand his question and share his interest, but do grant me a little deference to her tender years and be patient with me. Eventually I did come through.) Momentarily, at least, the probing inquiry had been ignored, but a deep sense of foreboding was warning me that I would be hounded by his question. The terrible moment of truth was very near, and it made my stomach hurt.

It was probably a month before the question was repeated. My son's interest was still high, though. He read his little book on occasion and even delivered small lectures on embryology to his sister. There were no questions for a while, and I was feeling fairly comfortable at home when (once again at mealtime) the monster bared its teeth.

It was a carbon copy of before. The same words, "There's something I don't understand." This time I said, "Uh-oh," immediately. I knew the terrain now and was already braced for what lay just over the next ridge.

"I just don't know how the sperm gets in there."

There was no getting out of it. For one thing, I had genuinely prayed for wisdom to answer my son, and I had prayed for the opportunity as well. I truly did want to help him. To make matters worse, one of my excuses was gone. The meal was finished, and his little sister, who was usually the last to clean her plate, was out of the room.

Gathering together all my reserved resources, I began. "Oh," I replied. That seemed inadequate, and after a moment of awkwardness and a quiet look of anticipation from my wife, I realized that it would be best if my explanation were more full.

"Well, you see [I spoke very calmly showing no ruffle], the sperm grows inside the daddy's body."

"I know, in his testicles" was the quick reply.

I took a drink of coffee and continued: "Well, you see, when the sperm leaves the daddy's body and gets inside the mommy's body [not thinking that the omitted specific details were necessary], it then travels through the tubes— remember the fallopian tubes?—all the way to what's called the ovary. That's where the two combine, and God creates what we call a zygote."

"Daddy, I know that part. You don't understand what I'm asking."

I had the very sure feeling that I did know what he was asking.

"See, I don't know what the daddy has to do to get the sperm out of his testicles and into the mommy."

"Oh," I said with an emphatic rising inflection. "That's what you mean." Well, will you believe that I copped out again? I simply couldn't do it! All my high principles notwithstanding, all my years of promising myself honesty with my kids, and now this. Craven fear. Ignore it and maybe it would go away. Maybe, after all, I was mistaken to have thought that it was so important anyway. He was only eight. Maybe it wasn't such a good thing to answer his question. He probably wouldn't really understand it anyway. Did you ever rationalize?

Well, you might imagine the consternation now plaguing me. Twice I had completely failed the big test. My son was asking the natural question. If I didn't tell him soon, he might determine that this business of how babies were made was something of which I wanted him to remain ignorant. Or he might suspect in time that I was ashamed of it (I remembered the apparent shame of my own parents, and the quietness about sex in my home). Furthermore, I knew that he was already being exposed to those careless sex words and games children play at school. It was hard to face, but he was already a third grader. As I remembered my own grade school experiences, I recalled that I had heard some of the dirtiest sex stories I ever heard in my life while in the third and fourth grades. I could still recall them in detail, so deep was their impression on my mind. The startling realization came to me that very soon my son would be learning about sex by reading rest room poetry and listening to the stories of the older boys at school. I knew I didn't want that.

At that point something significant dawned on me. Among the good reasons why my son should hear about sex from his daddy emerged what seemed to be the most compelling one of all. I wanted his very first impressions of sex to be entirely healthy ones. Before he heard some ugly toilet talk or jokes about girls; before he began to feel foolish because he didn't understand what they were talking about; before he became ashamed of being interested in the facts about sex; and above all, before he decided that his daddy was a poor source of information; before any of that, I wanted him to have heard it first at home. I wanted him to hear his daddy talk about it openly and honestly. I wanted him to know that sex was a blessing and a joy before he began to fear that it was a curse. I wanted him to know that sex was a method of giving before he heard that it was something boys could take from girls. I wanted his first knowledge of sex to be surrounded by the light of God before he heard it in the shadows of this evil world. It had to be now. I prayed, *God help me to do it right.*

God did help me, and I have always looked back on the night it happened with a deep sense of God's blessing. I will never forget it, and I will always thank God for giving me an experience of openness with my son that many fathers have never known.

My wife had gone to the hospital and had given birth to our second son. I was playing housemother in the meantime caring for the children at home. One night after his sister had already fallen to sleep, and just after I had heard his prayers, my son raised the subject once again, this time with a tone of growing frustration.

"Daddy, aren't you ever going to tell me how the sperm . . . ?

I sat down on the bed and looked at him. It was so hard to remember what it was like to be eight years old. He really was ready, and I was afraid. Yet, the moment had come, and I knew it. I whispered a quiet prayer for wisdom and began.

"Well, you know how when you really love someone, you want to touch them?"

"Yes, like when Mommy and you hug me?"

"That's right. Well, you see, God has created us like that. Our hearts are connected to our bodies, so that when we love somebody very much, we just want to touch them with our hands and hold them in our arms and sometimes kiss them."

"I know it."

"And it feels really good to hold someone close and kiss them, doesn't it?"

"Yes." His eyes were fastened on me with a look that showed deep interest and great confidence in Daddy's wisdom.

"Well, Son, God has made our bodies in such a way that when a man and a woman love each other very much, they can express this love with the whole body."

"Really?"

"Yes, they can. And when they do that, sometimes it causes a baby to grow inside the woman's body."

"Then, is that when the sperm gets inside the mommy?"

"Yes, it is." I knew, of course, what the next question was to be.

"But how?"

There was no way to make this easy. It had come right down to the basic, mechanical facts of sexual intercourse, and I was about to tell my son the facts. Why was it so tough? It was almost as if using the words would violate some sacred innocence. I feared to say the words, to name the sex organs, and to describe the coital union. Why was I so afraid? This was my son, eager to know, ready for the widening of the horizons of his life.

Perhaps the realization that my boy's horizons were about to be widened far beyond his own expectations—combined with the knowledge that sex could be full of pain—was causing me to somehow want to spare him the inevitable. Yet, I had to tell him. He would learn it all. And he would learn it very soon. If I failed him, he would hear it from the boys. No, this was my responsibility, my privilege, my business.

"Son," I began with a look he must have read as indicating that I was finally ready, since he scooted up into a half-sitting position.

"Son, when a daddy holds a mommy very close to him and kisses her and feels that he loves her very, very much, something happens to him that makes his penis get very hard and stand up straight."

"That's happened to me sometimes when I need to go to the bathroom."

"Sure," I said. "Well, it's like that when a man loves a woman, too. When the man's penis gets hard, then he can place it inside the woman's vagina."

At this point he giggled.

"Is that funny?" I asked.

"Uh-huh," he answered.

"Well, I guess it does seem a little funny when you talk about it, but it isn't funny when you do it. Really, it's a very wonderful experience."

"Does it hurt?"

"No, Honey, it doesn't hurt. It feels very nice, and it makes you want to love the other person even more."

"Then, is that how the sperm gets into the mommy's body?"

"Yes, it is. When the man pushes his penis inside the woman's vagina, soon the sperm comes out of his penis and flows into the woman's body."

He seemed very thoughtful for a moment. Then he said, "Golly, so that's the way."

"So that's the way," I affirmed.

I watched him intently. He was taking it in, and I wondered what he thought. Then the thought came to me. I did it! For better or for worse, I did it, and now he knew. He knew, and he had learned it from his daddy. Suddenly, I realized that all the suspense was gone. I had fared well, I thought. I had often heard that in instructing children about sex you should tell them only as much as they are asking, so it seemed to me it was time to quit.

"Well, then, do you think you understand now?"

"Yeah, I think so" came a quiet answer.

"Well, then, you'd better go to sleep. We will talk more about this some other time." I leaned forward and kissed him, then walked to the doorway.

"Daddy," he called.

"Yes."

"Don't your clothes get in the way?"

I was startled by the question. The wonder and excitement of the moment gripped me afresh. It was all old stuff to me, so easily comprehended, but a whole new world was dawning on my little boy. The clothes. Of course, what about the clothes? I turned and walked back to the bed, now with a little mist in my eyes.

("As a father pitieth his children . . . ?")

"Sweetheart, you take your clothes off," I explained.

"Oh, . . . yeah, sure."

"Now, do you have any more questions?"

"No, I guess not," he said.

Once again I headed for the door. Once again he called.

"Daddy."

"Yes, Honey."

This question came very hesitantly, almost reverently.

"Did you ever do that?"

Again, the wonder of the moment was gripping my heart.

"Yes, of course," I said. "Where do you think Mommy and I got you?"

"Oh, . . . yeah, and Sissy, too."

"Right, and Sissy, too."

"Golly."

"Now, you really need to go to sleep," I said. "We'll talk about it again, OK?"

"OK."

I walked to the door again.

"Daddy."

"What?"

There was a pause punctuating the moment.

"Thanks."

"You're welcome, Son."

"I love you, Daddy."

"I love you, too, Son. Good night."

"Good night."

I shut the door and walked down the hall. There were tears welling in my eyes and a lump in my throat, and somewhere in God's universe there were angels singing.

Golly, I thought to myself.